THE PRESENT AND FUTURE OF RELIGION

C. E. M. JOAD

THE PRESENT AND FUTURE OF RELIGION

ERNEST BENN LIMITED

1930

Made and Printed in Great Britain by
The Camelot Press Limited,
London and Southampton

CONTENTS

INTRODUCTION

The purpose of this book is threefold: to give an account of the state of religion in this country to-day, to analyse the reasons for its admitted decline, and to indicate the conditions which must be satisfied if it is to revive. The subject, it will be agreed, is far from simple. The complex of beliefs, ways of life, organisations, and institutions vaguely summed up in the one word "religion," presents such diverse and even contradictory phenomena that adequately to achieve any of the three objects which I have set myself would carry me far beyond the limits of the present book. The decline of religion belongs, indeed, to the history of our times, and to treat it with the fullness it deserves demands qualities of patience and scholarship to which the present writer can lay no claim.

The task, in short, is beyond me; nor have I attempted it. Apart from the fact that I have not the requisite qualifications for the compilation of an exhaustive work, my treatment of the subject is necessarily conditioned by the nature of my interest in it, which is that neither of a believer nor of a sceptic, but of an absorbed spectator. I neither welcome nor deplore the tendencies I have set out to analyse, but I find them intensely interesting. My standpoint—and I hope the admission will not set the reader against me—is, in short, that of the philosopher, interested in what people believe and anxious to discern the reasons why they believe what they do. It follows that my method of treatment is highly subjective. I have written about what interests me largely in order to make certain things clear to myself. Hence, while the first part of the book is in the nature of an impressionistic sketch, the second is, in effect, a statement of an individual philosophy; and, as the first makes no claim to completeness, so does the second make none to finality.

But, lest the apparent detachment of the foregoing remarks should lead the reader to think that I am a

superior person, who regards religious beliefs as
foibles which it is his business to notice but beneath
his dignity to share, let me hasten to add that the
writing of this book has proceeded from two deeply
held convictions. The first is that the need to believe
is fundamental, and that man's spiritual health suffers
if the need is not satisfied ; the second, that the religion preached by the Churches does not in fact satisfy
this need to-day, and is likely to satisfy it less in the
future. If, therefore, men are to regain the sense of
spiritual rest and the refreshment of spiritual stimulus, which only sincerely held religious belief can
give, one of two things must happen. Either a new
religion will take the field, which, not challenging the
modern scientific conception of the universe, is fitted
to appeal to the modern educated intelligence, or the
Christian Churches must cease to maintain propositions which are in flagrant contradiction with known
facts. This is not much to ask ; yet, if the Churches
were to comply, they would need so radically to re-
state most of the doctrines upon which they at present
insist as, in fact, to concede the demand for a new
religion.

Where so much is obscure, one thing, at least, is
certain : the interest in religion, an interest which
evinces itself in quarters where it might have been
least expected, has increased and is increasing. There
is a reaction from the indifferentism of the last few
years, and religion has assumed a place in the fore-
front of public attention. Religion is news ; it is even
best selling news.

Since it was announced some little time ago that this
book was in the press, I have received no less than
ten works upon various aspects of religion from
authors who have desired me to acquaint myself with
their views, and where, as has happened in one or two
instances, extracts from the book have appeared in the
form of articles in the Press, they have evoked more
correspondence than any articles I have written. In

general, the spate of books on religious subjects continues unchecked, and theology still ranks next to fiction as the most popular subject with authors. Thus there is a marked disparity between the decline of organised religion and the growth of popular interest. There is a twilight of the old gods ; yet, in spite of the popular demand, no new ones come to take their places. It is the desire to resolve this apparent contradiction that has been mainly responsible for the writing of this book.

Short extracts from this book have appeared in the form of articles in *Harper's Magazine*, the *New Leader*, the *Evening Standard*, the *Star Review* and the *Rationalist Annual*, and my thanks are due to the Editors of these publications for permission to reprint them.

C. E. M. JOAD.

Hampstead, 1929.

Part I : The Decline of Religion

Chapter I

THE DRIFT FROM THE CHURCHES

Chapter I

THE DRIFT FROM THE CHURCHES

Traditional formulæ have withered in the mental environment created by modern knowledge and been replaced by a wistful agnosticism.[1]

An annual return is prepared showing the number of those attending Sunday schools in the Protestant Churches of England and Wales. In 1927 it showed a drop of 122,762 scholars as compared with 1926. In 1906 the Anglican and Free Churches could claim 6,455,719 scholars ; in 1928 the number had shrunk to 4,748,872, a loss of over one and a half million ; while in that year alone the Anglican Church lost 19,977 scholars, and the Wesleyan Methodists 11,765.

In 1927 the Chairman of the Congregational Union of England and Wales produced figures showing that 25 per cent. of the six million public elementary school-children in England and Wales received no religious instruction outside their day-schools. He found, further, that of 10,000 children attending 50 element-ary schools, 50 per cent. of the boys and 40 per cent. of the girls did not even possess Bibles.

Coming to the adults, we find that a comparison be-tween records of church and chapel attendance in a typical London area with a population of over 80,000, at three different periods during the last sixty years, shows that in 1886–7 the total number of persons at-tending was 12,996, and the average attendance at 44 services was 295. In 1902–3 the total was 10,370, and the average at 56 services was 184. In 1927 the total was only 3,960, and the average at 62 services was 63. It is interesting to note that, as the numbers of the congregation have gone down, the number of the services has gone up.

[1] Extract from an open letter addressed by the Bishop of Bir-mingham to the Archbishop of Canterbury (1928).

An enquirer who has recently visited 134 churches at random reports the following facts. At 40 Free Churches the congregations varied from 200 to 6, with an average attendance of 40 at the morning services ; the attendance at 60 services in Anglican Churches ranged from 500 to 15, with an average of 55 in the morning and 101 at the evening services ; five 8 a.m. Communion services had an average of seven communicants. In a spaciously beautiful City church the clergyman preached to five men, eleven women, and five children. The services at St. Swithin's, Cannon Street, are attended by seven or eight people ; it is a fine church, and £50,000 has been offered for it by a business firm.

During 1926 a Bill was promoted in Parliament to dispose of 19 City churches declared to be redundant. Speaking for the Bill in the House of Lords, the Bishop of London said, " There are (in the City) 46 churches, with 60 clergymen, 46 organists and choirs, ministering to about 20,000 people at a cost of £50,000 to £60,000 annually. That is a scandal. A dozen churches would suffice, and £23,000 a year would be saved." The Bill was passed by the House of Lords, but thrown out by the Commons. It will be said that the population has withdrawn from the City and that the churches have been left in a backwater. This is true ; but it is not the whole truth. The East End, so far as I am aware, is still as populous as ever, yet in one East End district 11 out of 24 Protestant Churches have been closed in the last forty years.

It is difficult to over-estimate the importance of these figures. They mean that a generation has grown to maturity which our fathers would have regarded as profoundly irreligious, and that they would find us getting worse every year. If irreligious means indifferent to the appeal of organised religion and sceptical about the Christian cosmogony, we should have to admit the charge. Whether our indifference to organised religion means that we have no use for religion, in the sense that we do not feel the need of faith and do not suffer from the lack of spiritual experience, is another matter. Let us, however, see how far our disbelief carries us.

In October 1926 the *Nation* published the results of a questionnaire on the state of religious belief. The questions asked were searching ; they raised fundamental issues. Do you believe in God ? Do you believe that Christ was divine ? Do you believe that the Bible is divinely inspired ; that the first chapter of Genesis contains an historically accurate account of the creation of the world ; in personal immortality ? I do not propose to summarise here the answers[1] ; briefly, however, those who gave affirmative answers to these questions, the sort of answers, that is to say, which would be given by persons generally in agreement with the main doctrines of the Christian religion, numbered between 30 and 35 per cent. of the whole. The remainder were either agnostics or avowed atheists. The believers in *organised* religion as formulated in the tenets of a church numbered only 25 per cent. The *Daily News*, which shortly afterwards invited its readers to answer the same questionnaire, returned a poll of roughly 63 per cent. affirmative answers. Far more people believed that the Bible is inspired than that the first chapter of Genesis is historical. The inference seems to be that many people who regard the Bible as God's book consider that He has wilfully deceived His readers in the first chapter. In due course American newspaper readers were confronted with the same questions ; the returns showed an 80 per cent. majority for orthodox belief.

The inference is obvious : the *Nation* is read by the best educated classes in the community—by professors, by University men, by teachers, writers, scientists, and, presumably, by politicians ; the *Daily News* by the lower middle classes, not so well edu-

[1] They will be found in Appendix I., together with answers to the *Daily News* questionnaire.

cated, valuing respectability and anxious to do and
think the right thing.

The American figures, taken at their face value, are
sufficiently startling. But, on reflection, one is inclined to wonder what their face value is worth. Many
Americans who do not believe desire to be thought to
believe, and in a land which is notorious for irreligion
it is more than the position of any public man is worth
to profess doubt. Belief in God, moreover, like belief
in natural purity and prosperity, is sedulously boosted
by the Press, which is quite capable of suppressing
evidence pointing to a state of affairs other than that
which it makes it its business to profess to desire.
Certainly the answers to a questionnaire prepared by
the Institute of Social and Religious Research,[1] indicating the attitude of American students to compul-
sory attendance at religious services, do not suggest
that those who swell the congregations at college
chapels are animated by genuine religious motives.

Here, for example, are some typical answers :

"We do not think of it (i.e. of going to chapel) so much as a wor-
ship period. It is more of a get-together, and is a big influence on
campus life. All announcements are given there. One is afraid he
will miss something if he does not go."
A football coach in a small college for men remarked that
"chapel gets the students up early and started for the day."
"Most of the chapel talks are for raising money."
"It is mere discipline put on to get men out of bed."
"It is held for the sake of keeping men here over week-ends."
"It is a place for roll-call, announcements, and for visitors to
speak."

The answers from women's colleges were in the
same vein :

"All participated heartily in singing and general worship ; the
pastor from a town church preached and made a too evident effort

[1] See Chapter III., pp. 45, 46 for figures obtained by this institute, showing the effects of science upon religious belief among
American students.

to please; the room was very quiet; but all through the back girls
read novels, studied, chatted, or whispered. The fact that they
came prepared to while away a boring hour was evident."

In the more responsible American magazines articles
appear drawing attention to the growing irreligion of
the young. Since, it is urged, it is impossible to tell
what the youthful American believes in, it must be
presumed that he believes in nothing, a presumption
which is amply borne out by the account of the manners and morals of young Americans contained in
such a book as Judge Ben Lindsey's *The Revolt of
Modern Youth*.

It is not scepticism in the matter of religious belief
that these enquiries reveal, so much as a complete indifference to the whole subject.

There is no doubt that the general attitude of the majority of the
students in college towards religion is one of indifference rather
than of support or hostility. Everyone is pressed by work and outside interests, and many regard religion merely as an added com-
plication to, rather than a simplification of, life.[1]

The nineteenth century has been called the age of
belief; the twentieth the age of doubt. That we doubt,
and doubt increasingly, who, in the face of the figures
quoted above, would wish to deny? Yet it would be
wrong to think of our age as primarily an age of
doubt. For the distinction between doubting and believing does not go to the heart of the matter. Doubt
at least implies interest. But it is not so much the fact
that we doubt that is important, but that it is no
longer thought to be important whether we doubt or
whether we do not. In the nineteenth century one of
the first things you knew about a man was the nature
and intensity of his belief. For example, we are rarely
introduced to a leading character in nineteenth-
century fiction without being told of the religious

[1] Report from a women's university college printed in *Learning
and Living*, the thirty-fourth annual report (1928) of the Student
Christian Movement.

Br

organisation to which he belonged, and of the assiduity or otherwise of his church or chapel attendances—in George Eliot's books a man's religious denomination is almost the most important thing about him—and, if he did not believe at all, or belonged to no religious organisation, or belonged and did not attend, there is a great fuss. To-day you can know a man for years without knowing whether he is a Christian or an atheist, what Church he attends or whether he attends one at all. The question of belief or doubt, in short, no longer matters.

Usually he does not attend one at all. What is more, the younger he is, the more modern in his outlook and circumstances, the less likely is he to attend. In the 1929 election, the minister of a Wesleyan Church, formerly a Liberal, was converted to Labour. With the enthusiasm of the convert, he was anxious to help the Labour cause by using his pulpit to stress the intimate connection between Socialism and the teaching of Christ. To do so, however, was to invite economic ruin. The congregation of his chapel, upon whose offerings his stipend depended, were substantial elderly folk, Liberals to a man, who would have left the chapel if political opinions contrary to their own had been expressed. The young of the district, to whom the new minister's message would have appealed, never came near the chapel.

The new suburbs—those lines of pink-roofed villas and bungalows that spread over the countryside like an irritable rash, as though the land had been stricken with eczema—are almost without churches. For example, since the war there has sprung up between Sutton and Merton a new population of 10,000 with religious provision for about 400. Dagenham, which is already almost as large as Southampton, has the church and chapel accommodation of a small town, and even this is not fully used. These architectural monstrosities are inhabited almost entirely by young married people, complete with cars,

but without children. The men go to town daily by
the 8.50 and return by the 6.30, while the women
follow their example whenever they can spare the
money for a matinée, which is about twice a week.
They acknowledge no duty towards God, in whom
they do not believe, and no duty towards their neighbours, whom they do not know. Cut off from the life
of the spirit, keeping themselves to themselves, living
in one place and sleeping in another, they pass their
lives in perpetual transit from workshop to dormi-
tory. At the week-ends they take the car along the
main roads and glare suspiciously at other motorists.
They lack the strength of those whose roots are in the
soil ; they are deprived of the social pleasure of those
who live in a community, and they have no souls at all.

A hundred years ago, when one of the new towns of
the industrial revolution sprang up, men's first concern was provision for their religious needs, and, if
they were Free Churchmen, a levy for the chapel was
one of the first charges they felt called upon to meet.
To-day nobody spares the money to build new
chapels, for the same reason that nobody would attend them if they were built. As for the Church of
England, even if there were churches and congregations to fill them, which there are not, there would not
be enough clergymen to attend to the congregations.
It is difficult, indeed it is impossible, to keep up the
existing numbers of clergy, and the supply of recruits
falls off year by year. In the early years of the twentieth century there were some 21,000 clergymen of
all ranks at work in England. In order to maintain
that number it is estimated that 650 new men must be
ordained every year. In the ten years 1907–16 the
average yearly number ordained was 624 ; in the ten
years 1917–26 it had fallen to 306. As a result, the
present (1928) staff of the Church of England is
just over 16,000, and the number is still diminishing. Some resign in sheer discouragement—among
them the Rev. W. O'Connor, Rector of Hedgerley,

Buckinghamshire, who, in a public announcement
in the winter of 1928, gave reasons for his resignation
which are so pertinent to my present purpose that I
must be excused for briefly quoting him:

> There is only one reason for my resignation, and that is the feel-
> ing of depression and discouragement which has been growing on
> me for the last three or four years.
> There is in this parish a number of people who never enter God's
> house. There is a large number who enter it very rarely.
> What grieves me most is to see so many of the boys and girls fol-
> lowing the example of their elders and cutting themselves off from
> the means of grace.
> The worship of God is a trouble to them, and they seldom or
> never darken the door of His house. I have failed to influence
> them. I feel as if I were up against a brick wall ; and so I had better
> retire.

There are even cases, admittedly not of clergymen,
but of rich and pious philanthropists who bribe
people to attend divine service by gifts of money.
"Three thousand boys attended service at the ——
Institute last Sunday, and Mr. —— then announced
that, if the boys brought the number up to 5,000
next Sunday, he would give every boy a ten-shilling
note."[1]
On the following Sunday it was estimated that some
5,800 boys appeared. Beginning to queue up outside
the church at eight in the morning, the majority could
not be admitted until four hours later ; there was no
room. Ultimately it was found necessary to hold three
services one after the other, thus enabling all to qualify for the ten shillings.[2]
Keenly alive to the peril of the situation, the
Churches endeavour to distract attention by waxing
fierce over questions of dogma : whether bread and

[1] Taken from the *Daily News*, 24th January, 1929.

[2] Taken from the *Daily News*, 28th January, 1929. This episode
provides an interesting commentary on the comparative contemporary popularities of God and Mammon. It should, however, be
added that a number of clergymen made a public protest against
this method of filling the churches.

wine are bread and wine or something else, or whether
they both are and are not bread and wine at the same
time ; these are questions which, it seems, are difficult
to answer, but easy to resent. An eminent English
Bishop recently issued a challenge to all and sundry to
distinguish by tasting, touching, smelling, reducing
to their ultimate chemical constituents, or subjecting
to any other test, any difference between a consecrated and an unconsecrated wafer. The authorities
of the Church did not take up the challenge ; they did
not even insist upon the difference ; but they said
that the Bishop's remarks were most unfortunate and
had given pain to thousands ! There has been open
dissension in the Church, there has even been brawl-
ing in St. Paul's. In olden times kings who felt insecure upon their thrones blew up the flames of
foreign strife in order to distract men's minds from
trouble at home—the practice, by the way, has not
been altogether discontinued in our own times. It
almost seems as if the Church would reverse the
process, and embark upon strife within in order to
turn men's thoughts from the apathy without. The
Modernist movement in the Church has provoked a
concerted attempt to light the old fires of the heresy
hunters, but the wood, it seems, is wet ; it will not
catch.

For the decay of religion various causes are assigned. There is, first and foremost, the war. Our
generation has seen religion prostituted to the uses of
belligerent nations, and ministers of the gospel of
peace exhorting men to kill other men, whom they
were persuaded by the ministers of the gospel of love
that it was their duty to hate. The problem of pain
and evil has been forced with a new emphasis on
men's attention. It has seemed more difficult to believe that God was good and that virtue would be
rewarded in heaven ; and, as belief in the next world
decayed, nothing seemed to matter except the supreme importance of "having a good time " in this

one, a phrase which certainly did not denote the en-
joyments of the spirit. Material changes have acceler-
ated the drift from the Churches which the change of
heart had begun. There were Sunday games, there
was a new craving for the open-air, there were motors
to take the family into the country, and the family
itself, that solemn little church-going *bloc*, was break-
ing up. Finally, there was the spread of science. . . .
All these things have contributed to produce what
is vaguely called the spirit of the age, a spirit sceptical,
disillusioned, irreverent, impatient of authority, and
distrustful of dogma.

And yet, though the Bishops quarrel and the congregations fade away, though the Churches are seen
to stand for little more than a system of traditions
corrupted by time and brooding, and emasculated by
celibate fancies with which the essential humanity of
Christ is overlaid and obscured, though men in increasing numbers refuse to subscribe to orthodox
beliefs, the part which religion has played is not yet
done. There are signs, indeed, that it is taking a new
lease of life. Never have so many books been published on religious subjects ; never has the discussion
of the fundamental questions with which religion
deals been more vigorous ; never has there been such
a ferment of spiritual unrest. Noting these signs of
the times, the Press has not been slow to exploit them.
In recent years the papers have devoted an increasing
amount of space to a discussion of religious topics.
Under such titles as "Is there a soul ?" "Where are
the dead ?" or "What I believe !" fundamental religious issues are eagerly canvassed, and leading novel-
ists are invited to express their views on questions
that have provided the chief themes of theological and
philosophical discussion. Business men give their
views on the qualifications of Christ as an advertiser
of spiritual goods . . . Religion, in short, has become
news.

We should be on our guard against misinterpreting

this awakening of interest as a sign of well-being.
Men do not talk about their health when they are
well, but when they are sick ; we do not attend to our
bodies so long as they function properly. Discussion
is provoked by dissatisfaction, and controversy is
generally a prelude to change. For centuries we have
been wearing a particular suit of morals and subscrib-
ing to a particular set of beliefs. All the time we have
been growing, but the process of growth has been
for the most part too imperceptible to be noticed. In
recent years it has speeded up, and, in the form of a
spiritual discomfort which we can no longer ignore,
has forced itself upon our attention. Wondering why
we are uncomfortable, we find that the moral and
spiritual clothing that we have worn for so long has
begun to irk us ; it is ceasing to fit. And so we have
set about discarding it and looking for a new outfit.

Now the process of discarding beliefs that we have
outgrown, and finding new ones appropriate to our
more developed mental stature, is neither easy nor
pleasant, and it is only when stimulated by gross
spiritual discomfort that we are prepared to undertake it. The undertaking, moreover, provokes controversy and is attended with friction. It is through
such a phase that religion is passing to-day. There is
controversy within the Church itself, between the
exponents of different forms of Christian doctrine
and the upholders of rival practices, and there is
controversy between those who hold the Christian
doctrine in some form or other and those who, under
the influence of science, look to observation and experiment rather than to revealed religion for truth
about the universe, in short between believers and
agnostics. Both controversies react unfavourably
upon the traditional religion of the established
Churches. Finally, there is the complex of diverse
tendencies denoted by vague expressions such as
" modern unrest" or "the spirit of the age." How
far these are responsible for the decline in traditional

beliefs, and how far they are themselves the effects of that decline, it is difficult to say. A personal opinion is that "modern unrest," with all that the expression implies, is at once the reflection and the prop of the religious indifference the causes of which I hope to analyse. The decline of religious beliefs and the growth of the modern spirit are two aspects of a single process, and cocktails and jazz, promiscuity and suicides, the craze for pleasure and the lust of speed, are the expressions of tendencies which only they have made inevitable.

It is because the gospel of Christ is waning that the gospel of "having a good time" bids fair to supersede it ; yet the latter is in part responsible for the decline to which it owes its own strength. In the succeeding chapters I shall endeavour to give a brief account of the factors which have been chiefly operative in re- ducing organised religion to its present pass—namely, the controversy within the Church, the controversy between religion and science, and the tendencies loosely grouped together as expressive of the "spirit of the age."

Chapter II

THE DISINTEGRATION OF THE CHURCH

Chapter II

THE DISINTEGRATION OF THE CHURCH

The second main reason for the present alienation of educated men and women from the Church of England is the growth of erroneous sacramental doctrines.[1]

For God's sake don't touch the Church of England. It is the only thing that stands between us and Christianity.[2]

In the Church of England to-day there are, broadly speaking, three main parties. There are, first, the Anglo-Catholics. The Anglo-Catholics deplore, but are not surprised at, the declining influence of the Church. It is only, they are inclined to say, what we should have expected. The message of Christianity as interpreted by the strictly orthodox Church of England clergyman is, they affirm, as arid as its practice is uninspiring. So dry and dull an appeal cannot hope to compete with the thousand and one calls upon the modern man's time and interest, and, unless something can be done to infuse some life into the Church's creed and some warmth into its practice, it will within the next fifty years perish of inanition. Hence the Anglo-Catholic aspires to bring back to the Church some of the colour and movement, to recover some of the mystical ardours and ascetic discipline, that she lost at the Reformation. He would adorn her practices with the rich jewels of a beautiful ritual, pressing the arts of painting and music into her service, and decking her priests with the gorgeous vestments that become the representatives of the regal majesty of the Divine.

The Anglo-Catholics are mainly to be found among the younger clergy. They are men of tireless energy and of unmistakable sincerity, pre-eminent for their

[1] Extract from an open letter addressed by the Bishop of Birmingham to the Archbishop of Canterbury (1928).

[2] A contemporary wit.

whole-hearted devotion to their calling and the simple austerity of their lives. Go to an Anglo-Catholic church, preferably in some poor district in the East End of London, and you will no longer feel surprise at their influence. The warm colouring and emotional ardour of Anglo-Catholicism glow like a flame against the background of squalid streets and pinched lives. The tapers flickering on the altar, the slow silences and sudden bursts of sound, the tinkling bells, the incense smoke caught in the shifting light of a high-windowed building, the moving figures clad in robes of flaming colours, the procession, how can these things not appeal to the dwellers in narrow courts and fœtid slums, whose outlook is bounded by the sordid cares of poverty and disease, and whose souls, starved of beauty, welcome any gleam of colour to break the drab monotony of their lives ?

Of this elaborate ritual the Eucharist is the culmination as it is the core of the Anglo-Catholic's faith, and it is his attitude to the Sacrament of the Eucharist, which the ordinary Churchman calls the Holy Communion Service, that brings him into conflict with the orthodox party in the Church, and more particularly with the Evangelicals. The Evangelical is shocked at what he cannot help regarding as grossly improper overtures to the Scarlet Lady of Rome. He is conscious of the strides that are being made by the Anglo-Catholics ; he hears of churches where the Mass is celebrated, where confessions are made, and where, through the incense-laden air, the rich colours of an ornate ritual glow and sparkle ; and, horrified at this betrayal of the Protestant faith of his fathers, he fears lest all that has been gained since the Reformation may be jeopardised, if, indeed, it has not been already lost.

The questions at issue between the two parties have come to a head in a controversy about the practice of Reservation, and the controversy about Reservation

springs in its turn from a divergence of opinion about
the Eucharist itself. The orthodox doctrine of the
Church of England holds that the bread and wine
are by faith only the body and blood of Christ, and the
act of eating the bread and drinking the wine constitutes, therefore, by faith, for the ordinary Churchman,
his participation in the body of Christ. Roman Catholics, as everybody knows, hold that the wafer which
is consecrated in the Mass *becomes* the body and
blood of Christ, and it was largely upon this issue, the
issue of Transubstantiation, that at the Reformation
the Church of England seceded from the Catholic
Church of Rome.

The Anglo-Catholics do not in so many words subscribe to the doctrine of Transubstantiation, but they
sail very near the wind, and the service which pre-
cedes the consecration of the wafer in Anglo-Catholic
Churches is, in fact, very similar, and in some cases a
literal translation of that in use in Roman Catholic
churches. If, therefore, the process is effective in
working the miracle in a Roman Catholic church,
why should the same process be ineffective in an
Anglo-Catholic one ? That the Anglo-Catholics believe that it is effective, that the consecrated wafer
does in fact *become* the body of Christ, is, say the
Evangelicals, shown by their adoption of the practice
of Reservation. Reservation means putting aside some
part of the substance consecrated during the Communion Service—a service which in High Churches
is to all intents and purposes the same as the Catholic
Mass—enclosing it in a small box called a pyx sus-
pended in the church, usually over the altar, or in a
small cupboard in the chancel, called an aumbry, so
that this consecrated something, whether substance
or symbol, is always present in the church. I use the
word "something" non-committally, but, according
to the Evangelicals, it is no symbol that the Anglo-
Catholics wish to reserve, but the body of Christ itself. For why, they ask, should Anglo-Catholic priests

be averse from disposing of the remains of the consecrated wafer, unless they were in fact assured that it
was Christ's body ? Why should they wish to pre-
serve it, to ensure that it may be continually present
in the church, except for the purpose of praying to
it and worshipping it ? And it is precisely this worship of the Reserved Sacrament in Anglo-Catholic
churches, a worship that to their opponents seems
indistinguishable from the idolatries of Rome, that
is to the Evangelicals the chief cause of offence. And
not only to the Evangelicals, but also to the Modernists.

For there is a third party in the Church, a party
weak perhaps in numbers, but strong in intelligence
and prestige, including as it does most of the men of
first-rate ability in the Church. This is the party of
Bishop Barnes and Dean Inge. It is separated from
the great bulk of Churchmen, and especially from the
Evangelicals, by its open-minded acceptance of the
teachings of science and its willingness to revise, and
even to discard, outworn dogmas in the light of that
teaching ; but it sides with the Evangelicals against
the Anglo-Catholics on the issue of the Reserved
Sacrament. And it does this because, to enlightened
men, the elaborate ritual of the Anglo-Catholic
smacks unpleasantly of the mumbo-jumbo of the
savage. Has not Sir James Frazer shown conclu-
sively in *The Golden Bough* how primitive peoples
eat their god in order to strengthen themselves,
and is it really credible that the practice of eating
Christ's body and drinking his blood is not a direct
lineal descendant from this old anthropomorphic
ritual ? And what is the doctrine of the Real Presence
but a reversion to the superstitions of the Middle
Ages, an affront to the intelligence of educated men,
calculated to alienate from the Church those who
have any tincture of the modern scientific spirit.
Bishop Barnes has repeatedly referred to the Anglo-
Catholics' "magical or pagan" conception of the

Sacraments, and protested in the plainest terms that "mediæval theories rejected in the bluntest language at the Reformation are openly taught in Anglican Churches."

The English Church to-day (he has said) has only been narrowly prevented by the State from changes that would end in the primitive superstition that a priest can give spiritual properties to the inanimate.[1]

On the positive side Modernism stands for the humanising of religion, seeking to make it at once more personal and more topical. There is a growing insistence upon conduct as opposed to doctrine, conduct meaning conduct in this life, which is regarded as important for its own sake, without reference to its bearing upon our prospects in the next. Thus religion, instead of being confined, as it has been in the past, to a particular set of activities springing from an isolated and unique side of our nature vaguely conceived as spiritual, is extended to embrace every aspect of our personality, and introduced into all the avocations of daily life. Hence a new emphasis is laid on the social side of Christianity, and the Christian point of view is defined in relation to the business world and to industrial disputes.

The world, in other words, is out of joint. This is a matter of serious concern, since life in this world is important in and for itself ; but it is only by the application of Christianity to life that the evils of the world can be mitigated. The aspect of a man's religion, of which it is the business of the Church to take cognisance, is that which finds expression in the way he lives. His faith is his private concern, a matter of personal religious experience, and should not, therefore, be confined too closely within the bounds of any specific creed, or broken on the wheel of obsolete dogmas. In brief, the way a man lives is more

[1] Bishop Barnes, preaching in the City Temple in the autumn of 1928.

important than the precise details of what he believes. Thus far the Modernists !

The antagonism between the various parties came to a head in the struggle over the Revised Prayer Book. The Anglo-Catholics have contended that the practice of Reservation should be explicitly sanctioned, and the Bishops' proposals, rejected by Parliament, permit the practice in certain cases without enjoining it. While it was still doubtful whether the Revised Prayer Book might not become law, a mass meeting of the younger clergy among the Evangelicals decided that, if it did, they would neither follow its services nor obey its instructions. It has not become law, and the scent of disestablishment is in the air, while the Bishops are considering to what length they may go in disregarding the veto of Parliament. At the time of writing (summer 1929) Convocation has decided to authorise through administrative action the use of the 1928 Prayer Book, in spite of its decisive rejection by the House of Commons.[1] Meanwhile the practice of Reservation continues, and Anglo-Catholics cheerfully conduct services which it becomes increasingly difficult to distinguish from the Mass. And they are prepared openly to resist any attempt to interfere with them. The Bishop of London, for example, has in his communications with Anglo-Catholic clergy forbidden devotions directly connected with the Reserved Sacrament. He has refused to allow the Reserved Sacrament to be moved from its appointed place, the aumbry or the tabernacle to be opened or censed, or any reference to be made to the presence of the Reserved Sacrament in the prayers. At the time of writing, twenty-one incumbents in the London diocese have decided to contest the Bishop's ruling. "We wish to make it plain," stated the Rev. C. P. Shaw, who was chairman of the meeting at which the decision was taken, "that should we ever come to accept

[1] This Resolution was carried in the Upper House by 23 votes to 4 and in the Lower by 96 votes to 54 (11th July, 1929).

your lordship's interpretation of our oath of canonical obedience, we should at once lay down our ministry." Thus there is dissension in the Church itself and chaotic variations in the practices of individual clergymen, and it is difficult to see how the strife of the contending parties is to be composed. At the moment it seems probable that the Church will split into two factions.

It ill becomes a layman, perhaps, to comment upon matters of so technical a character, yet it is difficult to forbear. To him, as I suspect to the Modernist, the whole controversy presents itself as an idle wrangle of little men fussily intent on erecting a molehill into a mountain. On the one hand, he sees Christ, a heroic figure, knowing that He is going to die and sitting down to His last meal with His disciples. And knowing it to be His last and feeling a natural sorrow at the prospect of parting with those who have been with Him for so long, He looks round for something by which they may remember Him. And, seeing the bread and wine, the materials of their simple meal, He bids them, whenever they eat and drink in the future to think of Him. He would have them treat the bread and wine on the table before them as symbols, souvenirs as we should now say, of this last meeting—and that is all. On the other, he sees pedants and doctrinaires taking this simple natural thought and the noble utterance in which it found expression, letting it fall upon the sterile soil of their little minds, and raising therefrom this unholy crop of controversy and superstition and strife. Maybe he is a Socialist, keenly alive to the misery and suffering of mankind, persuaded that the misery and suffering are preventable, and believing that by a practical application of Christ's precepts they could be prevented. Maybe a pacifist, taking Christ's teaching on the subject of non-resistance seriously, and convinced that the only way to rid the world of war is for others to take it seriously too.

CR

Christianity, he will say, has failed only because it has never been tried. No State has yet made the beginning of an attempt to organise society on the assumption that the teaching of Christ is true. For many men of advanced ideas, to-day, Christ is primarily a great preacher and teacher of conduct, expounding doctrines of compelling force and originality. As such He despises ritual and ceremony, and lays stress upon what men do. He is a Communist and an internationalist, advocating the widening of the private family to include the whole family of mankind. He is a humanitarian, denouncing punishment, crying for mercy instead of vengeance, and insisting, if only as a utilitarian measure, on counteracting evil not with a contrary evil, but with good. Above all he is a Socialist insisting on the organic conception of society, and affirming that we are members of one another in so intimate a sense that the misery and degradation of one are the misery and degradation of all. Very well, then, to take Him seriously involves disbanding our armies, scrapping our navies, sacking our judges and lawyers, closing our prisons, and making arrangements for an equitable distribution of society's material goods. These things, no doubt, are difficult, and not to be accomplished in a day. You cannot inaugurate the Kingdom of God by Act of Parliament, but you can at least legislate as if you wanted to ; you can at least try. And because nobody does try, because nobody ever has tried, we have a civilisation in which the poverty, misery, and want of the many are outraged by the arrogance, luxury, and ostentation of the few, and a society which is not only based upon arrangements that violate every tenet of the creed it professes to hold, but prides itself on its readiness to defend these arrangements if they are attacked by organising public murder on a scale hitherto undreamed of.

Civilisation, it is clear, needs the practical application of the teaching of Christ as never before. It will crash, and deservedly crash, unless it tries Christianity before it is too late. And what are the Churches doing about it ? Troubled and perplexed by the difficulties of the times, we incline ourselves expectantly for their counsel and guidance. Our startled ears are assailed by a confused murmur, as it were the buzzing of angry wasps. We listen more closely, and the words "aumbries" and "reservation" distinguish themselves above the general clamour. The Churches, it seems, are very interested just now in the question of "aumbries." Or we hear a clerical voice rebuking a woman for entering a Church "uncovered"—that is, without a hat. St. Paul, it seems, said something about uncovered women in his first letter to the Corinthians. Or we are regaled with disputes about the Virgin Birth. The earth, we are given to understand, was visited some two thousand years ago by a man whose wisdom was so pre-eminent that it has seemed to many to partake of the divine. The Church, it is to be presumed, is the inheritor of that wisdom, or, if not its inheritor, at least its trustee. Reverently approaching, we ask that the teaching of this great visitor to our planet should be interpreted for us in the light of the needs of our times. And his trustees meet our request with a profound discourse upon how the distinguished personage travelled to visit us !

Is it any wonder that men feel a little impatient with the paid servants of Christ, and regard their wrangles over Reservation and the Virgin Birth as a clerical fiddling while Rome burns ? As the newly appointed Bishop of Chelmsford said, in his inaugural sermon, "While priest struggles with priest for the mastery, the world outside looks on with contempt and passes by on the other side." Some, no doubt, whether from traditional reasons or from sheer bewilderment in the face of the complexity of modern life, still look to the Church for light and leading. They look, but do not receive. For, where so much is uncertain, one thing at least is clear, that a Church rent by the dissensions and absorbed in the issues at which we have briefly glanced is in no position to give us what we need. "Men do really want help," said the Bishop of Salisbury, addressing a meeting of the Industrial Fellowship, "and they are not getting help from the Church, because the Church is divided." And so, though men still look for what it is the Church's business to give, they will soon look no longer.

Christianity has been a great adventure of the human spirit, and Christianity, it seems, in its organised and traditional form has failed. The consideration cannot fail to depress. As we read the lives of the founder of Christianity or of St. Francis, his greatest disciple, it almost seems, at times, as if the deadweight of human apathy and inertia might be overcome, and the bad old world made afresh. Hope is born, but only for a moment. Laying down our book, we remember the clergymen we know, and realise regretfully that Christ's dream of a regenerated world is too lovely for the little minds that run the machine of instituted religion.

Chapter III

THE IMPACT OF SCIENCE

Chapter III

THE IMPACT OF SCIENCE

One cause of weakness of the Church has arisen from the apparent determination of religious teachers to ignore scientific discovery.[1]

The part which science has played in promoting religious scepticism in the modern world is considerable ; science, indeed, has become a veritable stumbling-block to religion. Nor is the reason far to seek. Certain Christian dogmas in which members of the Church of England are required to believe are plainly at variance with what science has discovered about the nature of the universe. The scientific account of the universe is founded on observation, and can, in part, be tested by experiment, but the dogmas which this account contradicts are unsupported by evidence, and are believed, in so far as they are believed, solely on the authority of the Church. Hence arises a conflict between science and faith, a conflict in which the latter is so palpably at a disadvantage that Samuel Butler's definition of faith as the power of believing things that we know to be untrue seems increasingly to be justified. Forced to make a choice between the authority of the Church and the conclusions of science, intelligent men have little hesitation in preferring the latter. Hence arises a movement within the Church, known as the Modernist movement, which seeks so to interpret the dogmas of the Christian religion that they shall cease to conflict with the facts of science, and educated men may remain in the Church without having to leave their intelligences behind them every time they attend one of its services. This is the movement with which are associated men like Bishop Barnes and Dean Inge. Their standpoint implies a whole-hearted

[1] Extract from an open letter addressed by the Bishop of Birmingham to the Archbishop of Canterbury (1928).

acceptance of the conclusions of science. "Modern science," said Dr. Barnes, preaching at the City Temple in the autumn of 1928, "has constructed a wholly new scheme of the universe and man's place within it. . . . During the present century a wholly new student class has come into existence. The achievements and conclusions of modern science are now accepted everywhere among these new companies of students, not grudgingly, but with enthusiasm. . . . How to formulate a faith that shall satisfy the demands of science is the problem that to-day confronts the religious teachers of mankind."

" Your sons and daughters," said the Bishop of Gloucester, in a sermon in defence of Modernism, " at schools and colleges will be so trained that they will find it almost impossible to accept the old-fashioned view of religion. They will respect the reality of your religion, if it is taught in a way which does not commit them to uncritical or unscientific opinions."

The controversy between religion and science is not a new one ; it has raged more or less continuously since the publication of Darwin's *Origin of Species* in the middle of the last century. Briefly, what Darwin's theory of evolution purported to show was that the development of life upon this planet has been continuous. Once the earth had been too hot and too moist to maintain life ; it cooled, and the earliest forms of living organisms began to appear in the form of specks of protoplasmic jelly floating about in the intertidal scum upon the shores of the Palæozoic sea ; it grew cooler, and life left the water and, assuming a reptilian form, proliferated in the vast monsters of the Mesozoic age ; cooler yet, and there were birds and mammals. From one of these last, a small lemur-like creature, there were descended two collateral branches, one that of the anthropoid apes, the other that of the human race. Man, therefore, was not a special creation, but merely a late descendant of a long line that stretched back to the jellyfish and the amœba. Certain links in the chain were missing, but its main outlines were already sufficiently clear, and subsequent research has done little more than fill in the gaps.

This discovery came at first as a great shock. The doctrine of the Fall had taught men to believe that they were degenerate angels, and they were displeased to find that they were merely promoted apes ; unaccountably, I think, since to have risen from a lower form of life, however low, seems to be preferable to have fallen from a higher one, however high. Nevertheless, the blow to man's conceit was very great. The Church, however, quickly found means to salve the wound, by representing Darwin's process as a progress. Not only was man later than the amœba, he was also higher ; in fact, being the latest creature to arrive on the terrestrial scene, he must also be the last, the perfected product of evolution, a being made by God in the image of Himself. Whether the amœba would agree with this opinion is not known ; but until we are able to obtain the creature's views the case must go by default, since we are in the fortunate position of being both judge and jury in our own cause. It is we who assert progress, and it is about ourselves that progress is asserted. Have we not written all the books ?

But even if, as seemed only reasonable, the process from the amœba to ourselves were a continuous progress, how did it bear upon the Christian doctrine of the creation of the world ? The orthodox view was founded upon the chronology of Bishop Ussher, who maintained, in the seventeenth century, that the world was created in seven days in the year 4004 B.C. Even if the days were taken, as by many divines they were, to be not days at all, but periods of time of unspecified length, it seemed difficult to reconcile the period of 6,000 years which had elapsed since, according to the Bible, the world began with the length of time required for Darwin's process, and still more difficult to adapt it to the demands of the geologists. According to modern estimates there has been life upon the planet for roughly twelve hundred million years, and human life for about a million ; hence it will be seen that a very considerable prolongation of the seven days is necessary.

To meet the situation the Church adopted various expedients. Perhaps the most remarkable was that of Sir Edmund Gosse's father, according to whom the world had indeed been created in seven days, as stated in Genesis, complete with fossils, the fossils being inserted to try our faith and delude the scientists. The world, in fact, had been made suddenly by a number of separate acts of creation, but made such as it would have been if it had evolved slowly.[1] Why God should have wished to deceive us in this way is not clear ; so far, however, as I know, this view is not any longer held.

Again, it was a common Christian belief that, after the divine and semi-divine beings, man was the most important creature in the universe. It was unfortunate for this belief that Copernicus had in the fifteenth century destroyed the primacy of man's planet, representing it merely as an unimportant lump of matter, one among many, gyrating round the sun. But hitherto his primacy upon his planet had been unquestioned. Not only was he the centre of the

---

[1] A similar difficulty has arisen with regard to Adam's navel. Did Adam have a navel, or did he not ? If he did, then he was not the first man, since navels indicate mothers. Also, Adam was made in God's image, and there was a natural disinclination to attribute a navel to God. If he did not, then, since all other men have undoubtedly had navels, Adam was not entirely and completely a man. Therefore he was not the first man. One way out of the difficulty is to suppose that God created Adam complete with navel in order to deceive the physiologists. Adam, in other words, was created suddenly by a divine act, but created such as he would have been if he had had earthly parents.

earth's system, but it often seemed as if the rest of the planet were only there in order to put him in the centre, so readily had divines dropped into the comfortable habit of regarding the animal creation as existing merely for the purpose of ministering to the needs of man and providing edifying examples—as in the case of the bee or the beaver—for his children. Thus we find clergymen drawing attention to the goodness of God in giving rabbits white tails, in order to make them an easier target for human marksmen, a reflection which serves to illustrate a general tendency to value animals in proportion to their ability to flatter human conceit by simulating our qualities, or to sustain human bodies by permitting themselves to fall victims to our guns.

Man, as the most important creature in the universe, naturally represented the last word in created creatures—was he not made in God's image?—and no form of life could, therefore, supersede him, while the doctrine of the resurrection of the body assured his physical characteristics of immortality.

It is impossible in the light of modern science any longer to take this view of the human species. It is one among many, thrown up in the course of evolution, and probably destined to be superseded and sent to join the Mesozoic reptiles on the evolutionary scrap-heap, so soon as it has served the purpose of the force that created it, or life has succeeded in producing a species better suited to carry forward the process of evolution. A bishop of the Church of England[1] has himself envisaged the possibility that life, at any rate as it is manifested in human beings, may fail—a microbe, for example, may appear which is fatal to the human race—and the whole of our species may vanish from the face of the earth, as though it had never been. How are we to reconcile such possibilities with the coming of the Kingdom of

[1] Bishop Barnes in 1928.

God, which will presumably be permanent and perfect, among human beings upon earth ?

The bearing of the theory of evolution upon the
book of Genesis is an old story now, and I do not wish
to pursue further half-forgotten controversies. But
biology is by no means the only science that has
reached results that invalidate Christian dogmas.
There is scarcely a branch of scientific research in
which discoveries have not been made which are incompatible with the teaching of the Church, and the
more we learn about the material universe the more
false does the Church's teaching on matters of fact
and history appear. To anyone reading the Bible with
an unprejudiced eye, it is evident that its doctrines
are based upon and relative to the scientific ideas
prevailing at the various periods when it was written.
It is even possible to trace an advance in the science,
as in the morals, of the Bible from the Old Testament
to the New. Now the scientific ideas of two thousand
years ago have been exploded and superseded. We no
longer hold the biological theory of man as a special
creation, the astronomical theory of a solid heaven
and a fixed earth,[1] the chemical theory that bread,
water, and other objects can be changed into sub-
stances of a different order by special processes, or
the physiological theory that a substance called the
soul leaves the body at death. Why, then, should we
insist upon the literal truth of dogmas inspired by
these theories and bearing the marks of their origin
plainly upon them ? To do so puts a premium upon
incredulity and brings religion and all that it stands
for into discredit.

That this is in fact the effect of such insistence is
plainly shown by the results of a questionnaire
presented to American college students by the Institute of Social and Religious Research, in connection

---

[1] "Who laid the foundations of the earth that it should not be
removed for ever" (Psalm civ., verse 5).

with a comprehensive study[1] recently undertaken by that body into the morale of American under-graduates. The questionnaire was designed primarily to show the changes in the religious beliefs of students which occurred during the period spent in college. Reporting upon the effects of university study on the belief in the Bible, the investigators say :

In regard to changes in belief about the Bible, the largest groups were those who changed from a belief in the literal interpretation to a belief in the Bible as allegorical or ethical (men 30 per cent., women 35 per cent.), and those who retained unchanged a belief in the Bible as an historical record (men 43 per cent. ; women 38 per cent.) . . . Many made the definite statement that their study of science had caused them to revise their ideas as to the literal truth of the Bible, but they nevertheless considered it the foundation-stone of right living and practical religion.

Here we have a picture of a younger generation on the whole more conservative than British university students, who yet find their original and unmodified religious beliefs unable to withstand the impact of the modern conceptions of the universe with which their education has brought them into touch. That science, and particularly biology, is the villain of the piece is revealed by the following naïve answer to a question on the significance of the Bible and the authenticity of its stories.

Its significance has not changed, perhaps, because I am taking an engineering course and not one which deals with philosophy or evolution, I regard the Bible as history and as the word of God.

This is charming. There is vouchsafed apparently to simple engineers a happy faith in the Bible stories of the creation of the world, which is denied to those imprudent enough to study science or philosophy.

[1] The results of this study, which are exceedingly interesting, can be found in *Undergraduates, a Study of Morale in Twenty-Three American Colleges and Universities.* (Doubleday, Doran, & Company, Inc., $4.)

Particularly interesting were the answers to the questions about obstacles to religious belief. The largest single group (26 per cent. men ; 27 per cent. women) cited scientific courses as the most important obstacle.

But when every allowance has been made for the effect of the advances that have been made in the special sciences, in biology and geology, in physics and astronomy, in modifying man's outlook upon the world, it is the scientific attitude of mind in the most general sense of the word, an attitude which is the result of three centuries of experiment and discovery, that remains the greatest danger to orthodox belief. To analyse this attitude would take us beyond the confines of the present book. Describing it shortly, I should say that it consists in a new and a juster appreciation of what it is that constitutes evidence. A concrete illustration may serve to bring out my meaning.

I have recently been reading a book which describes the persecution of witches in Germany in the Middle Ages. The facts revealed are sufficiently startling even to those whose pride and pleasure it is to believe that they have no illusions about the credulity of mankind. They are briefly as follows :

In the space of about fifty years during the century immediately succeeding the Renaissance, no less than three-quarters of a million women were burned as witches in the area of Germany to which the researches of the author of the book relate. In many villages during this period there were no women left alive over the age of forty ; in others, the provision of the necessary faggots, tar, and pitch required for burning at the stake was found, owing to the frequency with which they were requisitioned, to be so burdensome a charge upon the finances of the community that roasting alive in an oven was substituted as being more economical. One oven, it was found, could be used for an indefinite number of witches.

The question immediately presents itself, on what grounds was such appalling suffering inflicted ? The town and village councils who condemned the alleged witches were composed of respectable burghers, not over-gifted with brains perhaps, but kindly and decent men, whose private lives were no doubt epitomes of all the domestic virtues. Such men would not pass judgment on malicious or frivolous grounds ; they would be satisfied that their condemnation was for the good both of society and of the witches, and that the evidence on which their verdict was based was unimpeachable. In point of fact they held that witches became witches through sexual intercourse with the devil, and that, unless they were made to confess and then burnt, their souls would suffer in hell the torments of the damned. The infliction of pain in the present was, therefore, a form of kindness to the witches ; it saved them from eternal pain in the hereafter.

But what about the evidence ? Nobody had ever seen the witches passing through keyholes, riding on broomsticks, or even having intercourse with the devil. How, then, was the evidence against them obtained ? The answer is simple : by their own confession.

The women admitted in every case that they had done these things, and they made this admission under the influence of torture. A woman suspected of being a witch was tortured and retortured (one woman was tortured in this way fifty-six times) until she reached a degree of suffering at which she preferred death by burning to being tortured again ; at this point she confessed. As part of her confession she was compelled to name her accomplices, so that each suspected woman became a centre of infection, from which there radiated an ever-widening circle of fresh suspects to be tortured and to implicate others in their turn.

These particulars of the methods of witch-hunters

in fifteenth and sixteenth-century Germany serve to illustrate a change which seems to me to have come over men's minds in the last three hundred years. And the change consists in this, that whereas it did not occur to the respectable German burghers to suspect the validity of confessions extorted by gross physical agony, no modern juryman would hesitate to stigmatise information so obtained as completely untrustworthy. What, in short, has come into the world is a certain respect for evidence, involving a capacity to discriminate between what is evidence and what is not, and this quickened appreciation of the nature of evidence is in a very large measure due to science, and to the peculiar temper of mind which science engenders.

Now I do not wish to assert that this respect for evidence is a permanent and universal characteristic of modern man. On the contrary, we are all of us still credulous for part of our time, and most of us are credulous for most of our time. That the average scientist in matters outside his own department is no more, and is often far less rational than the man in the street, a few minutes' conversation on politics with a scientific expert will quickly demonstrate. And, when we catch the infection of a war, we throw reason to the winds and tumble over one another in our eagerness to relapse into a state of mediæval credulity. In general it may be remarked that we become more credulous in proportion as the issues in regard to which our beliefs are entertained grow more important, the intensity with which we hold our beliefs being usually in inverse proportion to their truth. When the truth is known, as, for example, the truth that two and two make four, we do not embrace it with enthusiasm. Certainly nobody would be prepared to kill or to die for the sake of this probably true proposition. Where, however, the truth is uncertain, we supply the place of knowledge by converting other men's conjectures into dogmas, and then proceed to kill those who refuse to subscribe to the dogmas. The

history of religion is a history of persecution for the
sake of beliefs which there is no reason to suppose to
be true. Whether, for example, the Father is of a like
nature or of the same nature as the Son is a question
obviously incapable of precise determination, and
not, one would have thought, of great importance.
Nevertheless, men have killed one another in thousands, in defence of both these highly dubious
opinions.

In the light of the irrationality of the beliefs of man's
past, we must not expect too much from his present.
Fourteen years ago Germans believed that the English were wicked, that Germans alone were cultured,
and that God was a pro-German ; the English held
that the Germans were wicked, that England stood
for freedom and democracy, and that God was pro-
English. Each side embraced its own set of opinions
with fanatical intensity, but thought that the only
way to prove them correct was to kill off as many of
the opposing side as it possibly could. The Allies succeeded in killing more Germans than the Germans
succeeded in killing Allies, with the result that the
latter set of opinions are officially believed to have
been established—that is to say, the world has been
made safe for democracy and militarism has been
overthrown, with the result that at the moment of
writing we are enjoying military despotisms in Spain,
Italy, Hungary, Bulgaria, and Russia.

In spite of these aberrations the fact remains that,
when his emotions are not deeply engaged, the average man tends to require more evidence for his beliefs
than he used to do ; he is not so ready to take things
on trust, or, at any rate, not the same things. Credulous to a degree about Spiritualism and Christian
Science, he tends to demand of the old creeds that
they shall provide him with reasons why he should
believe in them, and, being a true child of his age and
therefore by disposition a materialist, he is inclined
to be unduly contemptuous of all evidence that would

DR

not be regarded as such by the physicist in his laboratory. Nothing exists, he is inclined to say, except those things of which his five senses inform him ; in other words, only material things exist. Such an attitude of mind, more often implicit than avowed, determines the approach of many to religion to-day, and it is small wonder that religion, judged by an arbitrary and often inappropriate test, fails to qualify.

Realising the danger to the whole structure of religion which science threatens, there are some within the Church itself who plead for a modification of religious dogmas in the light of our new knowledge, and urge that, in its own interests, the Church should not teach doctrines that conflict with the plain facts about the universe that science has dicovered. A *New Commentary on the Bible*, which appeared at the close of 1928, edited by Bishop Gore and published by the Society for the Propagation of Christian Knowledge, may be taken as representative of the more moderate school of advanced Christian thought.

Reviewing it, the Bishop of Liverpool pointed out that the Bible is, "rather a library of books, the writers of which, at various times and in various conditions of life, by divers pictures and in divers manners, declared their ideas about God and His dealings with man. . . these are not intended to be understood as narratives of fact, but as vehicles of teaching."

The plain meaning of this seems to be that the Bible is not "the word of God," but a collection of human writings embodying human and, therefore, fallible ideas. In other words, doubt of all religious dogmas is admissible, while some—namely, those which purport to be narratives of actual fact—must not be taken to mean what they say.

This is a considerable advance. The doctrines rejected by the *New Commentary* as "not intended to be understood as narratives of fact" have been insisted on with passionate emphasis as forming part of a supreme divine revelation. They include the Creation story, the Flood story, the stories of David and Goliath, and of Jonah and the whale. These, it seems, are not historical, are probably untrue, and form no part of a divine revelation. What are the inferences ?

(1) The Bible is a purely human production.

(2) The human mind is entitled to use its reason to determine what parts of it are valuable and what are not.

(3) The vast majority of Christian authorities have been mistaken

    (*a*) in claiming the Bible as divine revelation ;

    (*b*) in declaiming against Biblical criticism, which is now recognised to be our chief guide in determining which, if any, parts of the Bible are true.

A remarkable set of admissions from the leaders of an institution which for two thousand years has claimed superhuman authority ! It is a little surprising to find the "Commentators" accepting the bodily resurrection of Jesus on the ground that the evidence for it is "clear, sufficient, and convincing." The evidence for the Resurrection consists of a disputable inference from extremely uncircumstantial references to a supernatural occurrence made by unknown writers in a grossly superstitious age. The test of probability, moreover, which the writers have accepted as admissible in dealing with the Old Testament stories, is here abandoned, for, assuming the Resurrection to have been a real occurrence bearing witness to the supernatural government of the universe, one may well ask whether the supernatural agency responsible for the occurrence would, in fairness to the human race, have omitted to provide first-hand, unimpeachable evidence for so important an event. Or are we to suppose that God, whom Sir Edmund Gosse's father credited with the creation of fossils to bamboozle the scientists, is exhibiting the same mischievous humour in His mystification of the

Biblical critics ? It is scarcely probable, yet it is what
the "Commentators," under the sway of a pre-
formed theory of the divinity of Jesus, apparently ask
us to believe. And then there are the Christian dogmas of heaven and of hell. Are these retained ? It is
not clear, yet there is no doubt of their distressing
effect upon the modern mind. The Christian conception of hell it finds frankly revolting. Nor should this
attitude occasion surprise. It is said that Whitefield
preached men dead at his feet by his picture of the
torments of the damned, and even so recent a
preacher as the great Spurgeon emphasised the reality
of a physical hell. This horrible doctrine has always
been implied even when it has not been emphasised.
Even when the preacher did not explicitly threaten
his congregation, they would be reminded of the fate
that awaited them by some hymn telling them, for
example, how they were destined " to inherit bliss
unending or an eternity of woe." Of recent years it
has dropped into the background, but it is still there,
a skeleton in the cupboard of the Church's teaching,
whose bones can on occasion still be rattled to
frighten the wicked. But the world has repudiated it,
and in doing so has lost much of its respect for a
religion whose appeal was addressed largely to men's
fears.

And what of "the bliss unending" ? It has fared little
better, the modern man finding the Church's picture
of an after-life as unreal as it is unattractive. A more
boring sort of life for the average Englishman it
would be impossible to conceive. With no huntin', no
fishin', no motorin', no shootin', with nothing to
frighten and nothing to kill, above all with no little
round bits of matter to be fiercely or deliberately hit
with long, thin ones in the shape of bats, cues, clubs,
mallets, or racquets, a heaven so ill equipped cannot
—it is obvious—be expected to appeal to the tastes of
a sporting man. Women too are apt to find it lacking
in emotional colour.

The concepts of heaven and hell have played no little part in discrediting Christianity, and a religion that is to survive will have to jettison them as obsolete lumber. Yet the Church, if it does not insist on them, does not explicitly discard them.

The Bible, again, contains many statements of fact which modern science has, to say the least of it, rendered doubtful. Some of them are statements about the structure of reality, e.g. "The Holy Ghost proceeded from the Father and the Son" ; others about what purport to be historical events, e.g. "Jesus descended into hell." Is belief in statements of this type still made a test of faith ? It is not clear. The miracles, however, are retained, inadvisably, as it seems to me. And not only to me ; for Bishop Barnes and the more advanced among the Modernists openly avow the miracles to be one of the greatest stumbling-blocks to the acceptance of the Christian faith. In the circumstances their enthusiasm for the *New Commentary* is qualified.

"A recent commentary on the Bible in which Bishop Gore's influence has been paramount concedes evolution and seeks to retain miracles. The concession, which virtually no one disputes, undermines that authority of the Bible, on which the whole Anglican position is built." So Bishop Barnes, preaching in Westminster Abbey. The authority of the Bible being undermined, why insist on the miracles ? It is not clear. "The vast majority of living churchmen," the Bishop continued, "who have felt the influence of scientific method find miracles no aid to faith." A masterly example of the art of under-statement ! "That God can alter the mode of expression of His will no one doubts, but that He actually takes or has taken in the past such action is now generally doubted"—although not, apparently, by the Anglican Church as a whole, which still insists on the miracles as an article of faith.

The process of being rational about Christian dogmas is, it is clear, only in its infancy. At present its operations are irregular and its incidence capricious. If it is to save Christianity, it must—it is obvious—go further. Yet already it has gone too far, for the religious dogmatists who dominate the Church are giving nothing away, and zealots complain that the Modernists are betraying the citadel from within. Hence they are pressed for adherence to the strict letter of the Church's doctrines, the Incarnation, the Immaculate Conception, the Resurrection of the Body ; and, replying that these are symbolic truths, or that they should be interpreted in a spiritual sense, they are accused of being hypocrites and charlatans, seeking to remain in the Church, while disbelieving her doctrines. Part of the trouble is that many of the more intelligent clergy are in advance of their flocks. Confronted with the apparent fact, confirmed by Holy Scripture, that the earth is flat, and believing in their hearts that the stars are spangles of bright gold that will fall from heaven like a shower of hot hail at the Second Coming, simple congregations are confounded to find prominent men in their own Church bowing the knee to science, which denies these things.

Hence arises the demand put forward by the more conservative churchmen that men like Bishop Barnes and Dean Inge should either subscribe fully, openly, and literally to the Thirty-Nine Articles or should leave the Church. It is this claim to finality by the Church—a claim which means that the ideas of two thousand years ago are true absolutely, completely, and for all time—that is chiefly responsible for its loss of influence to-day. "We need," as the Bishop of Birmingham has said, "to re-fashion both dogma and worship by joining the spiritual intention of Jesus to the understanding of the universe. In fact, such a re-formulation of faith is the main duty of Christian leaders during the next generation." No doubt ! But it seems unlikely that the duty will be performed. Yet unless the Church can bring herself to let her most enlightened representatives move with the times, and, while retaining the spiritual message of Christianity, discard the outworn science of Christian theology, that influence will wane until it has vanished altogether. The Churches, no doubt, will continue to function for a time, but they will be attended increasingly, and in the end exclusively, by ignorant men, women, and children. Already a stranger attending an average Church of England service would almost be justified in assuming that the Churches, like theatre matinées, were kept up for the benefit of women and children. So far as present indications go, it seems not unlikely that science will deliver the *coup de grâce* to organised Christianity within the next hundred years. It is probable, however, that the services of the English Churches will still retain an interest for overseas visitors for many years to come, and it is quite conceivable that the Church, in company with the House of Commons and the Royal Family, may ultimately be subsidised as a picturesque survival by a syndicate of American millionaires sentimentally anxious to retain links with the past.

If by some miracle the Church regains its power, it will sterilise scientific thought and retard human progress by putting a ban on scientific experiment and discovery. This might not matter were it not for the fact that, as the world is organised at present, the result of the cessation of scientific research in Christian countries would be to leave us as defenceless against the non-Christian races, armed with science, as were the Asiatics against the Christian races in the nineteenth century.

Chapter IV

THE SPIRIT OF THE AGE

Chapter IV

THE SPIRIT OF THE AGE

The only way to get rid of a temptation is to yield to it.—O.
WILDE.

It remains to estimate the influence of "the spirit of
the age." The phrase is an ambiguous one, and its
meaning varies according to the context in which it is
used. As I understand it, however, it is intended to
imply a particular attitude to life—that, namely, of
most young men and women between the ages of
seventeen and thirty to-day ; and it is in this sense
that I shall use it. The attitude is complex and is the
product of a number of different factors. Three, I
think, may be specially distinguished, and I shall say
a few words about each of them.

There is, in the first place, the reaction on the part of
each generation from the manners and morals of the
last, a reaction which, in the generation which grew to
maturity in the early twentieth century, was more than
usually marked ; there is the influence of the new psychology in general and of psycho-analysis in particular, and there are the effects of the war.

And here I wish to anticipate a difficulty to which I
have already made a passing reference. These three
factors, and a number of others which I have not
specified, have contributed, I say, to produce a certain attitude to life, and this attitude, I hold, is one of
the causes of the decay of religious belief. But is the
word "causes" really appropriate ? Might it not,
ought it not indeed, to be "effects" ? And my difficulty is precisely this, that I do not know how far the
decline in religious belief and the apparent atrophy of
the religious sense are due, at least in part, to the
prevalence of an attitude to life which has grown up
concurrently with, but independently of, them, and
how far they have contributed to form that attitude.
Admittedly the two are inextricably interwoven, the

growth of the one assisting and being assisted by the decline of the other ; so that in describing, as I have tried to do in the next chapter (which has got itself written first), the effects upon contemporary morals and manners of the religious scepticism of the age, I find myself including among them some of the characteristics of the particular attitude to life which I am here asserting to be one of the *causes* of that scepticism. There is a vicious circle here, and those who seek to distinguish cause from effect do but perambulate its circumference. Because men's belief in the next world has declined, they behave in a certain way in this one, and the effect of their behaviour is to destroy the remaining vestiges of their belief. Thus men's creeds are at once the prop and the mirror of their lives, and reflect a morality which only they have made inevitable. But it is time to return to the "spirit of the age."

I. First among its constituents I have noted the reaction of the present generation from the morals and beliefs of the Victorian age. The inevitable repudiation by each generation of the standards and values of the last is a commonplace, and I need not enlarge on it here, except to remark that it goes some way to explain the repulsion felt by the twentieth century for the piety of the nineteenth. In all ages children have seemed to find in their parents warnings rather than examples, and have shown their sense of the effect of parental instruction by disregarding it to the best of their ability. Thus the sons of parsons become prize-fighters or take to the stage, while the children of Bohemians are remarkable for the ordered austerity of their lives. It is for this reason that old women and middle-aged men in every generation regard their youngers as immoral, irreverent, decadent, and sceptical, and inform each other that the world is going to the dogs, an expression by which they seek to convey their sense of protest against the movement of evolution for having passed them by. "When I was young,

Mr. Lydgate," says old Mrs. Fairbrother in George Eliot's *Middlemarch*, "there never was any question of right and wrong. We knew our Catechism and our duty. Every respectable Church person had the same opinions. But now, if you speak out of the Prayer Book itself, you are liable to be contradicted." Mrs. Fairbrother might have been speaking in the twentieth century : her period is, in fact, almost exactly a hundred years ago. Meanwhile, we may note in passing that each generation, in reacting from its predecessor, returns to the generation before its predecessor, thus taking the gods of its grandfathers off the shelf upon which its fathers have placed them. Thus we have the present enthusiasm for the eighteenth century, and strive to model ourselves in morals and beliefs, or rather in the lack of both, upon the intellectuals of the France of Louis XV. With, however, one important exception : in the age of Voltaire and Gibbon, the age of reason and logic, women tried to talk like men ; in the age of Freud and Bergson, the age of instinct and unreason, men try to talk like women.

II. The tendency to react from parental standards, operative in every age, has been intensified in our own by two factors of a somewhat special character. The new psychology in general and psycho-analysis in particular have had an influence upon the codes and conduct of the younger generation, the extent of which is not generally acknowledged. The general effect of the teaching of the psycho-analysts is to lead people to think that the springs of action are to be located not in the conscious, but in the unconscious part of our natures. Here is to be found the seat of individuality, the very centre and citadel of the self. Consequently the desires and impulses which appear in consciousness, proceeding as they do from the unconscious, may be regarded as the natural outcropping and expression of the self. But consciousness is also impregnated with other elements, which are derived not from the individual, but from his environment ; they are, speaking broadly, the reflection of the social codes and standards of the community to which he belongs. Society, said Schopenhauer, is like a collection of hedgehogs driven together for the sake of warmth. Naturally the spikes prick unless they are well felted ; hence arise manners and morals of which the function is so to felt the spikes of individualistic behaviour that the pricking is reduced to a minimum. The community being chiefly concerned to maintain a minimum standard of uniform law-abiding conduct among its members, the influence which it exerts upon the individual's consciousness takes the form of a series of checks and inhibitions upon the impulses which spring from the natural man within him. These are usually administered by the conscience, which is the policeman of society, implanted in the individual to safeguard social interests. Thus there is a continual conflict between the individual's natural and his social self, in which the latter endeavours to restrain the departures of the former from the currently accepted set of prejudices, preferences, and observances which the community pretentiously calls its morals. To take a personal illustration, I cannot abide the sight of a red-haired man wearing a straw hat, the impulse of my natural man being to hit the red-haired man violently in the face, to knock off the hat, or otherwise express my disapproval. But there is no social prejudice against the wearing of straw hats by red-haired men. Consequently my social man, schooled in the observances of the community to which he belongs and automatically reflecting them, reproves the idiosyncrasies of the natural man and sternly represses as anti-social any attempt to express them in action. Anti-social action may be defined as behaviour in a manner other than that which the community expects. This applies even to the unexpected answer : the Japanese term for a rude man, for example, is an "other than expected fellow," and, under the old laws, a noble is not to be interfered with in cutting down a man who has behaved to him in a way which he did not anticipate.

Now the successful repression of the natural man by the social man has, on the whole, been regarded in the main as a sign of advance. Man, it has been urged, chiefly differs from the animals in his ability to discipline and control his instincts in the interests of some end which he regards as valuable. Without such control society becomes impossible. Were we to bash the face of every red-haired straw-hatted man who annoyed us, capture and make away with every girl that attracted us, and appropriate the goods of our neighbours at the first opportunity, the ordered security of society would relapse into the anarchy of the jungle, and intercourse between individuals would be indistinguishable from intercourse between nations, which still, on the whole, conforms to jungle ethics. Now society is an achievement ; in it and through it alone a man may develop his tastes and realise all that he has it in him to be. Hence whatever threatens the stability of society has been regarded with disfavour, and the efforts of the individual's social man to suppress the aberrations of his natural man have usually had the support of public opinion.

Owing to the influence of psycho-analysis, the view that this suppression is desirable is no longer held with its traditional force. The impulses and desires which appear in consciousness spring, as we have seen, from the innermost source of our being. Now, every individual has, it is said, a right to complete self-expression. What is the purpose of democracy if it is not to give him that right ? But the right is not respected by asking him to starve one side of his nature in the interests of a code of morals to which he has never subscribed, designed to secure a social good in which he feels no interest. He has also a right to psychological health. But the writings of Freud have told him that, if the *libido* is suppressed, his personality will suffer. The stream of impulses and desires, the spontaneous uprush of his ego, which finds its natural outlet stopped, is turned back upon itself, stagnates, and spreads into a rank and fœtid marsh. This marsh is the complex, a terrible affair which poisons and infects the whole personality, with the result that the victim pays in hysteria, depression, and neurosis the price of the suppression and distortion of the desires of his youth. The moral is self-expression and self-development at all costs ; give free play to every side of your nature, and don't be deterred by the Mrs. Grundys of society from the experiences which the unfolding of your personality demands.

From the ethical point of view all indulgence is commended except indulgence in self-restraint, and we are urged to get rid of our temptations by yielding to them.

The doctrine of self-expression, to which psycho-analysis has given pseudo-scientific countenance, does not exhaust the effects of modern psychology upon contemporary creeds and codes. There is a markedly deterministic strain in the writings of modern psychologists. It is suggested that our actions proceed not from the conscious activities of will and reason, but from deep-seated forces within ourselves whose genesis escapes detection and whose workings evade control. But, if this is so, we cannot be held responsible for what we do.

Nor are the workings of these forces confined to their effect upon our actions. They dominate equally our beliefs, which are merely rationalisations of our instinctive wishes. Hence, we are not responsible for what we believe, nor, which is more to our present purpose, for what we disbelieve. This conclusion begets an attitude fatalistic as regards action and sceptical as regards thought. Since we cannot help doing what we do do, to tell us what we ought to do is an

irrational impertinence. Hence, we may as well do
what we like. Since we believe what we do, not because it is true, not even because we have examined
the evidence and think it true, but because we are predisposed in favour of the belief in question by our
wishes, and biased by our temperaments—because, in
other words, we are made that way—to advance arguments or to produce evidence in favour of a belief is a
waste of breath.

I shall examine in more detail in the next chapter
the practical bearing of this repudiation of moral and
intellectual responsibility upon people's actions and
beliefs. Meanwhile, I shall try briefly to show how
the conclusions of modern psychologists lend it countenance. Let us return for a moment to psycho-
analysis.

The plan of the psychological interior of the individual drawn by the disciples of Freud may be likened
to that of a two-floored tenement. The first floor is
inhabited by a quiet, respectable family, poor but
honest, dull but decent, anxious to keep themselves
to themselves, but determined to put up a good show
before their neighbours. Upon the ground floor, or,
if you prefer it, in the basement, there lives a much
larger family, dirty, untidy, primitive, obstreperous,
and licentious, devoid alike of decency and restraint.
Possessing to the full the snobbishness inherent in the
lower orders, this basement family is continually striving to raise itself in the social scale, and, partly for
this reason, partly from love of scandal and desire for
publicity, is desperately anxious to get a footing on
the first floor and to mix with the company to be
found there. Alarmed and scandalised by these des-
perate attempts, the first-floor people hire a sort of
guardian or policeman, and station him on the stair-
case in order to prevent the access of undesirables to
their floor. Sometimes the policeman succeeds in
keeping the basement people down ; sometimes he is
not strong enough to withstand their uprush. In this

ER

latter event, however, he usually succeeds in cleaning up the invaders *en route*, washing their faces, blowing their noses, giving them clean collars, brushing their clothes, and generally making them fit for company. So respectable do they indeed become that they scarcely know themselves in this new guise. If we call the first floor the conscious, the basement the unconscious, and the guardian on the stairs the censor, we shall recognise in the cleaning-up process what is known by psycho-analysts as sublimation, which may so completely disguise the character of the unconscious wish which appears in consciousness that a man's unconscious desire to elope with a waitress may appear in consciousness as a sudden aversion from pickled cabbage.

Now the uprush of these desires from the unconscious to the conscious is a completely unconscious process ; so far as consciousness is concerned, we can neither prevent nor control it. In order to control the events which occur in the unconscious, it is at least necessary to know what these events are. But, if we knew them, the unconscious would not be unconscious, but conscious. It is true that a resistance is put up to our unconscious desires by the censor, and a struggle ensues, which may result in suppression and usually results in sublimation. But of this struggle on the stairs we are again not conscious, and for its outcome we are not, therefore, responsible. It seems, therefore, that we cannot be held responsible for the desires that appear in the conscious ; we are accountable neither for their strength nor for their character. We cannot, therefore, be praised or blamed for the conduct upon which, under the influence of these desires, we embark.

Fatalistic conclusions of this type are by no means confined to psycho-analysis. They are implied in most modern psychology, though they are rarely drawn by psychologists. Let us consider for a moment a theory which bulks largely in psychological text-books—

Professor McDougall's theory of instinct. Professor McDougall begins by defining an instinct as "an inherited or innate psycho-physical disposition, which determines its possessor to perceive, and to pay attention to, objects of a certain class, to experience an emotional excitement of a particular quality upon perceiving such an object, and to act in regard to it in a particular manner, or, at least, to experience an impulse to such action." The upshot of this in non-technical language is that an instinct is part of our initial temperamental make-up, the psychological stock-in-trade which we bring with us into the world, the very seat and citadel of our individuality.

The form of its expression will, of course, vary according to circumstances, upbringing, and so forth, but the instinct which is expressed is the same in all of us. McDougall holds that there are thirteen separate instincts which may be defined in this manner, and these instincts, with the thirteen primary emotions, each of which accompanies an instinct as the peculiar emotion belonging to that instinct, constitute when taken together what may be called our personal or inherited, as opposed to our acquired, psychology. For this initial psychological endowment it is clear that we are not responsible ; we possess it, or, rather, we possess the potentiality for it at birth, and in reaction to the environment in which we find ourselves it develops and becomes explicit, until in due course it crystallises into what we call our personality.

The instincts are, according to McDougall, the source and origin of all our activities. On this point he speaks definitely and emphatically. "The instincts are the prime movers of all human activity ; by the conative or impulsive force of some instinct, every train of thought, however cold and passionless it may seem, is borne along towards its end. All the complex apparatus of the most highly developed mind is but the instrument by which these impulses seek their satisfaction."

Now we are all familiar with that view of people's motives which assigns to the reason the function of handmaid to the desires. It is desire which sets the ends of our activities, which determines, in other words, what we want, and reason which plans the steps which are necessary for its attainment. This function reason performs not only in the practical sphere, but also in the theoretical ; it not only tells us, in other words, how to do what we want to do, but assures us that what we want to do is right and that what we want to believe is true. The reason of David, for example, indicates to him that the way to get hold of Bathsheba is to get rid of Uriah ; it also informs him that Uriah is a very excellent soldier. Thus reason invents pretexts for what we instinctively wish to do, and arguments for what we instinctively wish to believe. That is why, though all men are presented with the same data on which to form a judgment about the relationship between this world and the next, they succeed in holding so many different beliefs. We believe what we believe, not on the basis of the evidence, but because we desire to believe it ; we also find it necessary to believe that it is the evidence which has constrained our belief. Savages who have not brought their reasons to the degree of perfection common to civilised men are not under this necessity of deceiving themselves about their motives. When the savage wants to go to war, he goes to war ; he does not find it necessary first to persuade himself that he is fighting for liberty and democracy. Not being reasonable, he is enabled to indulge his instincts without hypocrisy.

Now, I am not here concerned either to assert or to deny the correctness of this view of the relationship between instinct or desire and reason. All that I wish to do is to point out that it follows necessarily from McDougall's account of the function of instinct. According to that account, the reason is merely a piece of mechanism ; it is the engine of the personality, and desire is the steam that sets it going. Since it can accomplish nothing by itself, since it cannot even begin to operate on its own initiative, it follows that it can come into action only at the behest of instinct, its master. It is only natural, therefore, that, when it does get under way, it should travel along the lines which its master has pointed out to it.

Let us consider the bearing of this conclusion upon the so-called moral faculties. Let us suppose that Mc-Dougall's view of instinct as the prime mover of all human activity is correct, and proceed to apply it to the will. The philosopher Aristotle used to liken the psychology of the individual to a team of horses engaged in drawing a chariot under the control of a charioteer. The horses are wild and unruly, and each of them is anxious to go his own way irrespective of the wishes of the others. Unless, therefore, the driver were to keep them under strict control, the chariot would follow the pull of the strongest horse at the moment, or, rather, its course would be a resultant of the different directions in which all the horses were pulling at that moment, without actually following any of them. In any event, the driver would be incapable of keeping to a straight course in a given direction, so that, instead of arriving at its destination, the chariot would pursue a haphazard, zigzag path, swaying from side to side, if not overturning altogether. In order to prevent this, the charioteer keeps a tight hold on the reins and refuses to give any of the horses his head. This does not mean that he suppresses them altogether, but that he allows to each one only so much of his way as is compatible with the satisfaction of the others and the necessity which the chariot is under of completing its course.

Translating this analogy into the terms of human psychology, we may say that the horses are our individual instincts or desires. Each individual desire is purely self-regarding, and, provided that it can obtain satisfaction for itself, takes no thought for the

welfare of the rest. But besides these individual
desires there is also a desire for the good of the whole,
that is to say, the charioteer, which keeps the individual desires in check, constraining them to dovetail
their imperious demands and harmonising them in
such a way that no single desire shall obtain more
satisfaction than is compatible with the welfare of the
human being as a whole. It is this desire for the good
of the whole which is called the will.

The argument sounds, I fear, more convincing than
it is. If we consider this account of the will in the light
of McDougall's theory of instinct, we get the following result : Either the will is itself a form of desire or
it is not. If it is not, it is clear that it cannot be
brought into operation unless we desire to exercise it.
It may be true that we can use the will to suppress
inconvenient longings, but we can do so only in
so far as we first want to suppress the longings because they are inconvenient. Translating this into
McDougall's language, we may say that, unless we are
instinctively moved to use the will to suppress instinctive desires, the will is helpless. Either, then, the will
is itself a form of desire, or it is something which depends upon desire for its operation. But, if the will is
only another kind of desire, or is dependent upon
another desire, it is clear that it must take its chance
along with the other desires. If I desire to stay at
a night club and get drunk, but also desire to go home
to bed because my conscience tells me that night
clubs are wicked, or because I think I shall have a
headache to-morrow, we may, if we like, call the
second desire the will to suppress the first one. But
that should not blind us to the fact that, like the
night-club desire, it is itself a desire, or at least depends upon desire, that a conflict will take place between the two desires in which victory will go to the
stronger, and that what we actually do is determined,
therefore, by the strongest of our various desires at
the moment. But for the strength of our instincts and

desires we are not responsible. It seems to follow that we are not responsible for what we do. We are determined, in short, not by forces external to ourselves, but by forces and impulses—call them instincts, desires, or what you will—that lie deep down at the well-springs of our nature. This may seem to many a less humiliating belief than that of the nineteenth-century materialists, but it is not free will. What is more, it effectively precludes free will.

The bearing of all this upon morality is sufficiently obvious, nor can it, I think, be doubted that the practical fatalism in matters of conduct in which these theories issue is a potent ingredient in "the spirit of the age."

III. The third special factor in the modern attitude to life to which I wish to draw attention is the influence of the war. The war, while directly violating every principle that the religion of the nineteenth century professed to regard as sacred, swept men of every age and creed off their feet in a common wave of enthusiasm. It was then discovered that the one thing which can effectively unite men is the one thing that they all know to be wrong. But, in spite of this knowledge, they nevertheless affirmed that it was right, invoking their religion to sanction their desires by one of the most remarkable pieces of hypocrisy by which men's unscrupulousness has imposed upon their credulity.

Knowing and affirming that might is not right, they nevertheless acted as if the only way of demonstrating the justice of your cause was to kill off as many of the other side as you possibly could. If your killing was more extensive than that of the enemy, you were said to have achieved a victory, which was held in some mysterious way to demonstrate your superior moral virtue. Knowing that killing is wrong, they nevertheless insisted that an exception has been made in the case of people you have never seen, whom you killed by order of the State. Knowing and believing

in the Christian religion, they nevertheless impris-
oned many of those who drew attention to the teaching of Christ, and endeavoured to act in accordance
with it. And so on, and so on.

These proceedings, which are no doubt very natural
on the part of a people at war, are not calculated to
impress a critically minded younger generation with
the moral sincerity of its elders, especially when it
finds that it is expected to fight in the war that its
elders have made. In the last war the young men
suffered in the trenches while the old men uttered
moral platitudes in the background, an allocation of
functions which was not calculated to inspire the
young with respect for the old, or to cause them to
pay much attention to the platitudes. As a conse-
quence, the war has brought a disrespect for authority of all kinds. The old men, we feel, have made a
terrible mess of things and then proceeded to cover
it up with moral sentiments. Whatever we do, we
cannot do much worse, and we might as well cut out
the moral sentiments. Hence, the very fact that
morality, self-discipline, and restraint are enshrined
in tradition and enjoined by authority is a sufficient
reason for regarding them as suspect and throwing
them to the winds.

In Anglo-Saxon countries there is a remarkable confusion between moral and ethical questions as a
whole, and that comparatively small part of them
which is concerned with sexual behaviour. So deep-
seated is this confusion that for many people the
word "morality" means simply "sexual abstinence."
Owing to this confusion, a revolt from the standards
and ways of thought of the Victorians has taken the
form of a repudiation of sexual restraints. If the war
unmasked the values of the Victorians, if it showed
their morality to be hypocrisy and exhibited their
religion as a series of conventional formulæ, why
bother with such people any longer ? It is clear that
their boasted virtue can have been no virtue at all, for

look at its results ! And, looking at them, the young
go in for an extensive course of "sleeping around."

Similarly with regard to religion. The Victorians believed hard in God and went to Church in shoals.
Their God was—it is clear—a vindictive, jealous old
gentleman, a tribal deity, grossly, partial, and ad-
dicted to blood, especially German blood. Against
such a God the young emphatically protest. "If,"
they say, "there is such a Being—and we hope there
is not—we certainly cannot worship Him. Still less
can we bore ourselves by stuffily praising Him in
church. It is a fine day. Let's go out in the car."

Chapter V

THE RESULTS

Chapter V

THE RESULTS

People to-day want a gospel for life, and only too often they are not given it.[1]

The Press has recently devoted a considerable amount of space to cases of suicide among the young. These have attracted attention because they appear to proceed less from any concrete, assignable cause than from a general dislike of existence as such. A girl throws herself out of a window because she is tired of life ; a young man, the son of a sergeant in the Salvation Army, seeks death under the wheels of a tram because he can no longer reconcile his experience of the world with what he has been taught to believe. The English call those who kill themselves insane, and puzzled coroners, accustomed to pronounce upon those temporarily "maddened" by financial troubles or thwarted love, refer these voluntary deaths proceeding from affairs neither of the pocket nor of the heart to abstractions such as "the unrest of youth," or "the spirit of the age."

It is no spiritual *malaise* peculiar to the atmosphere of England that is responsible for these occurrences. On the contrary, the evidence seems to show that we in England are being visited by an epidemic whose ravages, extending over the whole of Western civilisation, have so far touched us but lightly. "Suicide epidemic among American students," says the morning paper, and proceeds to tell us that suicides among students had at the time of writing been at the rate of one a week for the past eight weeks. None of the deaths recorded were due to external causes, but to what is ambiguously described as "mental trouble." "Mental trouble" appears to resolve itself in one case into a frustrated love affair, in another into drug-

[1] The Bishop of Gloucester's Presidential Address to the Church Congress, 1928.

taking, into a clash of beliefs in a third, and into being bored in a fourth. "The student XY," we are told, put his head in a gas-oven "because he was 'tired of the girls' and didn't know what to do with himself." And so on.

In Berlin the death-rate by suicide among young men under twenty-five is reputed as high as one-tenth per cent. The Germans, it should be remembered, take their ideas seriously. For Russia, where they take them not only seriously but extravagantly, so that one does not so much have ideas as suffer from a rush of thought to the head, no precise figures are available, but the government are understood to have taken severe measures to prevent people killing themselves, presumably by punishing the offenders with death !

The epidemic seems to have been occasioned by an outbreak of thought consequent upon the breakdown of traditional beliefs. I do not mean to suggest that thinking about life necessarily leads to the conclusion that life is not worth living. Far from it. Upon the comparative merits of being alive and being dead the philosopher, indeed, is required to keep an open mind. Socrates, about to drink the hemlock, rebuked his friends, who advocated escape, pointing out that, as we do not know what being dead is like, there is no ground for the assumption that it is worse than being alive ; it is just as likely to be better. Hence, a reasonable man will neither seek nor avoid a state whose merits or demerits, compared with those of his present existence, are unknown to him. But this is less an argument for suicide than against a craven fear of death.

It is, however, true that it is upon the most intelligent that life bears most hardly. Schopenhauer went so far as to assert a natural incompatibility between intelligence and happiness. The more complex the human mechanism becomes, the greater the chances that it will go wrong. Refinement of the spirit brings greater sensibility to pain, while increased capacity for thought enables us to perceive illusions the more readily. The intelligent man finds it hard to believe, harder still to find an ideal which, by winning the respect of his intellect, can claim the allegiance of his heart. Throughout the history of philosophy runs the antithesis, "Which would you sooner be, Socrates dissatisfied, or a pig satisfied?" with the implication that it is harder for Socrates to come by satisfaction than for a pig.

That those who kill themselves are usually men and women of exceptional intelligence should not, therefore, occasion surprise. But young people have been intelligent in all ages and yet consented to live. What, then, are the reasons for the abnormal crop of suicides in our own? They are, I think, very largely to be sought in the lack of religious faith and feeling whose causes I have been analysing.

The effects of the decay in religious belief make themselves felt in two ways. In the first place, men are left without guidance as to the ultimate nature and purpose of the universe, and the status and destiny of the human spirit. Nor can they easily direct themselves. The average man does not make his religion any more than he makes his morals for himself. He does not even compare the various alternative systems of religions and morals that others have made, and choose the one which suits him best. He gets his religious and ethical beliefs, as he gets his boots and clothes, ready made from the social shop, upholding Christianity and monogamy instead of Allah and polygamy, as the result of circumstances which are, in the last resort, purely topographical. That I believe in God the Father, God the Son, and God the Holy Ghost (if I do) because I happen to have been born in a London bedroom and not in a forest hut or a Chinese palace is a reflection prejudicial to the dignity of the human mind, and is, therefore, rarely made. It is true, nevertheless.

Now, there are times when the spiritual clothes that our age purveys tend to misfit. In this respect, as I pointed out in the first chapter, the generation which has come to maturity since the war is unfortunate. Most of what it has traditionally been taught about the nature of the universe and the destiny of the soul is, as we have seen, at variance with what science has discovered and with a plain reading of its personal experience. The discomfort produced in an earnest and sensitive mind by this discrepancy between the dogmas which it has been taught to believe and the facts of which it is informed by experience and education may be very acute.

Most men have a need to believe. They like to be told what to think and what to do ; that is why the Church and the Army have always been their two most popular institutions. So intolerable is it for them to have to think things out for themselves that they are willing to regard any dogma as embodying the last word in absolute truth, and any code of morals as constituting a final and unquestioned criterion of right and wrong, if it is presented to them with a sufficiently authoritative backing. What is more, they will be prepared, if put to it, to defend the code and the dogma to the last ounce of their energy and the last drop of their blood, regarding it as the height of wickedness to act and think otherwise than in accordance with them, and inflicting appalling cruelties upon all who venture to do so. That the Holy Ghost proceeds from the Father and from the Son, or that he proceeds from the Father only, that bread and wine are or are not body and blood, or that in some mysterious sense they both are and are not at the same time, are propositions in defence of which men have killed one another in thousands, and practised hideous tortures upon thousands.

The need to believe is—it is obvious—very intense. Men lack the courage to gaze into pain, evil, death, and the deserts beyond death with their own eyes ; they need to look through the safe and misty glass of legend and dogma. The human mind, like a creeping plant, demands a support to which it may cling and upon which it may grow, and, finding it, embraces it with fierce intensity. The discomfort occasioned by the absence of such a support is none the less keen because its source is seldom realised.

Now the age in which we live is peculiar in that the supports it offers are not such as to sustain the weight of the contemporary mind. Coming to us from the remote past, they are simple in structure, unsure in their foundations, and unadapted to the complexities of the modern intellect. Thus the mind searches in vain for a substratum of what can be taken for granted upon which to rest. Not strong enough as yet to stand alone, it tends, unsupported, to give way under the strain. It is not altogether in irony that suicides are called "temporarily insane."

In the second place, scepticism about the universe leads to the adoption of a way of life which is apt to be found unsatisfying. Where everything is uncertain, the doctrine of let us eat and drink, for to-morrow we die, at once concrete and definite, is eagerly embraced. The future being unknown, it is the part of wisdom to make the most of the present that we know. At the same time, moral considerations, deprived of their supernatural backing, lose their accustomed force. We should be good, we used to be told, because goodness is pleasing to God. He loves an upright man ; He also likes him to be temperate and continent. Once the practice of virtue is identified with pleasing God, it becomes difficult to ignore the respective consequences of His pleasure and His displeasure. Most religions have taken care to paint these consequences in the liveliest colours, with the result that it is difficult to say how much so-called virtuous conduct has been prompted by the desire to achieve an eternity of celestial bliss, and to avoid an eternity of infernal torment.

FR

It is notorious to-day that heavenly rewards no longer attract and infernal punishments no longer deter with their pristine force ; young people are frankly derisive of both, and, seeing no prospect of divine compensation in the next world for the wine and kisses that morality bids them eschew in this one, take more or less unanimously to the wine and kisses. Unfortunately the pleasurable results anticipated from these sources fail to materialise. That unchecked indulgence in the more obvious types of pleasure is unsatisfying is the unanimous teaching of those who have had the leisure and opportunity to try them in all the ages. It is the more unfortunate that it is a truth which nobody believes to be true, until he has discovered it for himself, and there are some who in making the discovery fall out in disillusion and disgust.

Thus the religious indifference which determines the attitude to life of young people issues in a practical Epicureanism, which finds in "Let us eat and drink, for to-morrow we die" the only acceptable guide to conduct. Such an attitude, whatever it may mean for a mature sage, involves for the youth of the twentieth century a contemptuous abandonment of those inhibitions and restraints which the nineteenth century complacently termed its "morals." Now, I do not wish to uphold Victorian morals ; on the contrary, I think them stupid, cruel, and narrow, and the lives of those who were governed by them were thwarted and exasperated lives. But it is part of my contention that man has not yet evolved at a level at which he can successfully conduct his life without some canons of conduct to which his moral instinct bids him adhere, so that, even when he ignores them, he can feel that he does so at his peril, knowing that he might have done right when, in fact, he has done wrong. From this point of view almost any morals at all are better than no morals at all. A life without morals tends to be a life without duties, and a life without duties is apt to become by process of exclusion a life devoted to pleasure.

Now, as I have hinted above, the search for pleasure is exposed to one very serious drawback ; it fails to achieve the desired result. The knowledge that pleasure may not be pursued directly forms part of the instinctive wisdom of the ages, which the modern world has somehow missed. The kingdom of happiness, like the kingdom of beauty, is not to be taken by storm, any more than it is to be purchased with dollars. Pursue happiness directly and you will find that she eludes you ; but she will sometimes consent to surprise you, when you are busy with something else. Of this fact there is no adequate explanation. You may say, following Schopenhauer, that life is a restless, ever-changing urge, expressing itself in a continual series of needs and wants. Wanting is a pain, and provokes the individual to take steps to satisfy the want. Satisfaction brings pleasure, but only for a moment, since the old want is immediately succeeded by a new one. Now, since satisfaction consists merely in deliverance from the pain of need, and since, when it is satisfied, the need ceases, it is clear that the pleasure of satisfaction can only be momentary. Pleasure, in other words, is relative and dependent upon a preceding need, and does not outlive the need whose satisfaction it attends. Hence those who seek to live a life of pleasure make a double mistake ; they endeavour to obtain pleasure without undergoing the pain of the preceding need, and they endeavour to prolong pleasure, whose nature is fleeting, with a view to its continued enjoyment. But in proportion as pleasures increase, the capacity for them diminishes, since what is customary is no longer felt as a pleasure. The penalty we pay for these mistakes is restlessness, boredom, and satiety. This, at least, is the gospel according to Schopenhauer. Nor can its topical application be doubted. Senor Federico Beltran-Masses, taxed with painting the most sensational and sensuous

pictures exhibited in London during the summer of
1929, is reported to have replied : "I want my pictures to have a moment of electricity in them. Only
so can they express the new age. The cocktail is
necessary to the new life. People are bored and nervous, and the cocktail is the only drink that stimu-
lates them. I try to express this nervousness of the
twentieth century. I want to electrify people."

Or, if you like a more picturesque explanation, you
may say that the elusiveness of pleasure is one of the
penalties of the Fall, and that, since man left Eden, it
has been decreed that only by roundabout means and
by looking the other way shall he gain what most he
desires ; or, more picturesquely still, that God is a
practical joker, who created the world for the amuse-
ment derived from contemplating its anomalies. The
Tantalus joke is a good one, and the spectacle of
happiness being withdrawn from the clutching hands
of those who seek to grasp it does not pall even when
the play lasts through eternity. The irony is increased by the behaviour of the tantalised, who,
buoyed up by the hope eternally frustrated that the
future will be better than the past, praise the Author
of their miseries and express their gratitude that He
has not made things worse.

But, whatever the explanation of the coyness of
pleasure, the fact is undeniable. It has been discovered and rediscovered by successive ages, until it
has come to form one of the secular commonplaces of
worldly wisdom. The case is admirably put by one of
the characters in Mr. Aldous Huxley's exquisitely
penetrating social satire, *Point Counter Point*. A dis-
carded mistress, rusticating in the country, has expressed surprise that, having lost her lover, she
should yet be happy. Old Mrs. Quarles comments as
follows :

"It's because you're not trying to be happy or wondering why
you should have been made unhappy, because you've stopped
thinking in terms of happiness or unhappiness. That's the enor-

mous stupidity of the young people of this generation," Mrs. Quarles went on ; "they never think of life except in terms of happiness. How shall I have a good time ? That's the question they ask. Or they complain, Why am I not having a better time ? But this is a world where good times, in their sense of the word, perhaps in any sense, simply cannot be had continuously, and by everybody. And, even when they get their good times, it's inevitably a disappointment—for imagination is always brighter than reality. And after it's been had for a little, it becomes a bore. Everybody strains after happiness, and the result is that nobody's happy. It's because they're on the wrong road. The question they ought to be asking themselves isn't, Why aren't we happy, and how shall we have a good time ? It's : How can we please God, and why aren't we better ? If people asked themselves those questions and answered them to the best of their ability in practice, they'd achieve happiness without ever thinking about it. For it's not by pursuing happiness that you find it ; it's by pursuing salvation. And when people were wise, instead of merely clever, they thought of life in terms of salvation and damnation, not of good times and bad times. If you're feeling happy now, Marjorie, that's because you've stopped wishing you were happy and started trying to be better. Happiness is like coke—something you get as a by-product in the process of making something else."

Without some system of morals to discipline his passions, some guiding principle in obedience to which to conserve his energies, some channel of endeavour along which to canalise his efforts, a man's activities tend to become diffused, and his life purposeless. He achieves nothing, and grows tired and discouraged through lack of achievement. "The singular fact remains," said Nietzsche, "that everything of the nature of freedom, elegance, boldness, dance, and masterly certainty, which exists or has existed, whether it be in thought itself or in administration, or in speaking or persuading, in art just as in conduct, has only developed by means of the tyranny of arbitrary law." "The essential thing 'in heaven and in earth' is, apparently, that there should be long *obedience* in the same direction ; there thereby results, and has always resulted in the long run, something which has made life worth living ; for instance, virtue, art, music, dancing, reason, spirituality."

In most ages religion and the sense of moral obligation have provided the necessary discipline of which
Nietzsche speaks. Lacking both, the men and women
of our time find it, if they are fortunate, in work. It is
for this reason that the modern man is the hardest
worker the world has seen. He cannot afford to be
idle. For those who have no God, servitude to work
is of all forms of bondage the least, as servitude to
pleasure is the most exacting. Throw yourself body
and soul into your work, lose yourself in an interest,
devote yourself to a cause, lift yourself out of the selfish little pit of vanity and desire which is the self by
giving yourself to something greater than the self,
and on looking back you will find that you have been
happy. Pursue happiness directly, and it will elude
you ; purchase it, and it will turn to dust and ashes at
your dollars' touch.

We must work, then, we moderns, for work's sake,
and take happiness for the wild flower that it is. To
stabilise the rainbow, to bottle the perfume, to grasp
in order to possess, this is the prime error of the age,
an error which vitiates our lives and ruins our leisure.
Happiness is not a house that can be built with
hands ; it is a flower that surprises you, a song which
you hear as you pass the hedge, rising suddenly and
simply in the night, and dying down again.

For those who can work then, it seems, the case is
not so bad. But it is rarely in the modern world that a
man can chance upon employment that is more than
a monotonous routine of boring duties. It is not such
work that can endow his life with significance and
provide him with a substitute for the discipline of
morals or religion. And so he joins in the search for
pleasure.

The practical acceptance of Hedonism as a philosophy of life is facilitated by the psychological develop-
ments to which I referred in the last chapter. The
belief in the efficacy of the unconscious has combined
with the disbelief in the efficacy of God to abolish

ethics. Morality is doubly suspect. The incentive to act rightly because it is pleasing to God is removed by scepticism as to His existence; the incentive to act rightly, because we ought to do good for its own sake, is destroyed by the practical fatalism of the new psychology. If a man can act only in the way in which the strongest impulse of the moment dictates, there is no point in telling him that he ought to act in some other way. If we cannot act freely, we cannot act morally. The word "ought," said Bentham, if it means anything at all, ought to be excluded from the dictionary, while the whole concept of good is divested of meaning, and therefore of objective validity, by an analysis which exhibits it as merely a rationalisation of those of our impulses which happen to secure the approval of other people.

The effects of this attitude upon traditional ethics can be presented in their clearest light by considering their bearing upon that well-known Victorian faculty, the conscience. Conscience, once so popular and so respected, has gone out of fashion; it is become so *démodé* that men confess to possessing it with a kind of shame. What has happened to conscience, and why?

To answer this question, let us see what precisely the Victorian conscience was. The Victorians believed that the moral well-being of the soul was guarded by a vigilant and beneficent faculty known as the conscience. The conscience acted as a sort of "barmaid" to the soul. Faced with the fact that human beings, being fallible, must be permitted a certain amount of rope, she would countenance up to a point (and rather reluctantly, perhaps) the indulgence of their desires. But only up to a point! When that point was reached, "Time's up, gentlemen," she would say; "we close at 10.30; no more drinking now,"[1] and proceed to close the bar. If gentlemen

[1] I am writing only of English consciences as I know them. Another metaphor would now have to be invented to describe the activities of the American conscience.

continue to drink after closing hours, they get into
trouble with the law ; conscience, in other words, to
revert to nineteenth-century language, would proceed
to give them a bad time. This process was known as
suffering remorse. It was not suggested, of course,
that conscience was always successful in her inhibi-
tory activities ; she often—especially if you were
wicked—failed. But, even then, you had to pay a price
for her defeat ; she could always take the sugar out of
your coffee, even if she could not prevent you from
drinking it.

Now, it is clear that if the arguments indicated in the
last chapter are correct, this way of regarding the
workings of our moral interior must be given up.
Conscience herself, according to modern psychology,
is but the slave of some instinct (or the effect of some
stimulus) of whose workings we are and must remain
ignorant. If that instinct is stronger than the desire
that conscience admonishes (or the will suppresses),
then conscience (or the will) triumphs, and we are
considered to be virtuous (or persons of strong character). If not, the desire obtains its gratification, and
we are considered to be wicked (or persons of weak
character). But we are not in either case responsible
for what happens, simply because the part of ourselves that we know and can, therefore, control is not
the part that matters.

This psychological fatalism issues in a practical
repudiation of ethics, and convicts moral effort of
futility. The state of mind so generated is, as I have
tried to show, intimately bound up with the decay of
religious belief. Moral scepticism is at once the parent
and the offspring of religious scepticism. Both issue in
a disavowal of values. Religious scepticism tells us
that we have no ground for supposing that the universe is not, as it appears to be, a pointless collocation
of atoms, in which human life travels an alien
passenger across an indifferent environment. Life,
in fact, is a casual phenomenon, thrown up by the

haphazard process of evolution, a process which is itself without a goal. One day—when, for example, the heat of the sun is no longer such as to maintain conditions suitable for living organisms upon the earth—life will disappear from the one tiny corner of the cosmic stage upon which it has played its un-called-for part. The universe, then, is without pur-pose and without value ; the attempt to penetrate its mysteries is futile, for it has none ; the desire to apprehend its reality is doomed to disappointment, for there is no reality other than the world we know.

Moral scepticism informs us that the object of living is to gratify our desires. Goodness is a meaningless expression, or, rather, it has meaning only in terms of human desire : things are good because we approve them ; we do not approve them because they are good. In any event, we can only approve of what we like ; we cannot help what we like, and we cannot help acting in accordance with our likings. Therefore, even if good had some objective meaning, which it has not, even if certain things were valuable independ-ently of our desires, which they are not, we should not be free to pursue them.

Both lines of thought issue in the same conclusion. Nothing, it appears, is worth taking trouble about ; the universe is not worshipful and no elements in it are worshipful ; therefore there is no point in taking trouble about that. Morality is not valuable, for there is nothing to do but to gratify our desires, and, even if there were, we could not do it ; therefore, there is no point in taking trouble about that.

Thus scepticism in matters of belief, and fatalism in matters of conduct, go hand in hand. Together they combine to produce the state of mind from which spring the philosophical suicides with which the present chapter began. This state of mind determines the instinctive attitude to religious questions of many young people to-day. They are not hostile to religion ; they simply ignore it. They find the questions with which religion and morals deal meaningless ; to discuss them is merely boring. Stevenson says somewhere that the only three subjects worth discussing are love, freedom, and immortality. Living to-day, he would find a world in which not only are freedom and immortality not discussed, but in which it is not understood how they ever could have been discussed. I have been asked by students how a man of Stevenson's good sense could say such a silly thing. As to love, of course, the position is different.

Having in mind the writing of this book, I recently tackled a chance gathering of a dozen young men and women on the subjects with which it deals. Did they, I asked, believe in God. If they did not, did they ever feel the need of religion, and wish that they did. To the first question they answered "No" without exception. No one had believed since he or she had grown up. One only answered the second in the affirmative, and the recurrence of her occasional need was regarded by all, including herself, as tending to the discredit of religion. She felt the need of divine comfort and guidance, she said, when she was weak, ill, or in trouble. "Quite so ! " said the others. "That is what religion does. Its appeal is to your weakness, not to your strength. When you are ill or depressed, when you are below your usual form and unable to stand up to life, that is when it gets hold of you. That is why it has had such a vogue among the poor and the oppressed, the failures and the neuropaths. God, in short, only gets the men and women life doesn't want. Religion is a spiritual drug for the spiritually diseased. Healthy people do not need it." And, drawing attention to the historical importance of religion, emphasising the hold which it has exercised over men's minds in the past, and expressing a doubt whether what had been said constituted a complete account of it in the present, I was met by frank incredulity. Religion, it was asserted, is thought to be important merely because it has always been thought so. Its importance, in other words, is conventional, not real. It is a legacy from humanity's past, to which men pay the conventional respect due to unwanted bequests, a toy from the childhood of the race, which adults will discard.

And so I return to the starting-point of my first chapter—religious belief is rapidly and palpably on the decline. Young people in particular are either indifferent to religion or hostile to it. For the first time in history there is coming to maturity a generation of men and women who have no religion, and feel no need for one. They are content to ignore it. Also they are very unhappy, and the suicide rate is abnormally high.

Part II : The Prospects of Religion

Chapter VI

WHAT RELIGION IS SUPPOSED TO BE

Chapter VI

WHAT RELIGION IS SUPPOSED TO BE

Beware of the man whose god is in the skies.—BERNARD SHAW.

In Part I. I have tried to give an account of the state
of religion as it is in this country to-day. From this
account two conclusions have emerged. First, organised religion as it is embodied in the creeds of the
orthodox Churches has lost its hold, and is unlikely
to regain it. Secondly, men and women have nevertheless a need of religion. This need is a fundamental
fact of our natures ; human beings have it because
they are human beings, and they will continue to
have it so long as they remain human beings. To it
the religions of the past have ministered, and to it the
religion of the present does not minister. The inference is irresistible ; those elements in our nature
which have previously found satisfaction in religion
are at present thwarted and unsatisfied. Seeking to
express themselves, they are unable to find an adequate mode of expression, and, in so far as one side
of their nature fails to find an outlet, the men and
women of the twentieth century fail to grow up into
complete and fully developed human beings. They
are thwarted and repressed in respect of their religious
needs, just as their fathers and mothers were thwarted
and repressed in respect of their sex needs. To find
satisfaction they must find a religion in which they
can believe.

What, then, are the conditions with which such a
religion must comply ? This is the question with
which the second part of this book will be concerned,
and to which I shall try, however tentatively, to give
some sort of answer. Before, however, I can hope
successfully to approach it, two further questions present themselves. First, What is religion ? Is it, for
example, a particular set of beliefs, and, if so, what
beliefs ? And secondly, How does religion arise, and

what is the origin and nature of the need to which it ministers? With these two questions I propose briefly to deal in this and the succeeding chapters. I shall seek to show first that the set of beliefs which are commonly regarded as constituting what is called religion to-day are not such as to command the respect of the educated mind, and, secondly, that to locate, as many do, the origin of the religious need in the emotions and fears of primitive man, though it may throw some light upon the nature of that need, is not to explain its present character as a factor in the consciousness of civilised men and women.

First, then, What is it that religion is commonly supposed to be? Posed with this question, the ordinary man of the world would, I think, find some little difficulty in replying. As I do not want to embark upon a discussion of the varieties of religious belief by enumerating the different forms which religion has assumed during the history of civilisation, I shall assume him to have been brought up in twentieth-century England as a member of a Christian Church. This procedure is the more legitimate, since the comparative study of religious beliefs has shown that the fundamental tenets of all the great religions bear a strong family likeness; to all intents and purposes, indeed, most of them are the same, which is only to be expected, since the need from which they spring is the same need. Returning, then, to the average member of a twentieth-century Christian Church, I should expect him to reply somewhat as follows: "Religion is a belief or set of beliefs about the nature and government of the universe, and the status and destiny of human life within the universe. This belief or set of beliefs is to the effect that this earth, and all that lives upon the earth, were created by a God who is both omnipotent and benevolent—that is to say, both all-powerful and all-good. In spite of His omnipotence, He permits to us His creatures a measure of free-will, in order that we may mould our destinies by our

actions, and He suffers pain and evil to exist in order
that our natures may be disciplined by suffering, and
that we may learn to avoid what is bad. Because we
have not succeeded in doing this as well as might have
been expected, He has been constrained, out of His
great love for the world, to send His only Son into it,
in the guise of a man, to show people how they ought
to live, and to assure them that, if they succeeded in
living correctly—i.e. believed what He told them,
repented of their past sins, and avoided future ones—
they might be translated into Paradise and continue
there indefinitely in the enjoyment of God's company." It is, moreover, usually held that pain and
evil will disappear when our natures have been sufficiently perfected by suffering to make us fit to enter
the celestial world—i.e. the world inhabited by God
—although, should we fail in the test, we shall be
doomed to suffer pain and to perform evil eternally.
In spite of this latter belief, it is also held that pain
and evil are unreal in some sense in which happiness
and goodness are real. The reason for this is that it is
not thought to be compatible with the goodness of
God that He should create pain and evil which possess any reality other than that of mere seeming ;
they are, in fact, illusions born of our finite and partial
understandings, although the understanding by
means of which we realise this truth is, presumably,
neither partial nor finite. In general it is held that life
as a whole, and human life in particular, is not meaningless, but purposive, and that, although its purpose
may not be clear to us in the present, it will be revealed probably in an existence of a different type in
the future.

The religious person, further, has faith. The use of
the word "faith" means, I take it, that the above propositions—or propositions of a similar character—are
and should be based, not, like scientific theories, on
concrete factual evidence which can be brought forward in their support, nor like mathematical proposi-
GR

tions on rational arguments by means of which they can be irrefutably demonstrated, but on some inner feeling or intuition which can, and in many cases does amount to a conviction of positive certitude. Being modern, however, we like to have evidence for what we believe, and when we are asked to take our beliefs on trust, that is, to have faith, we like to think that we are committing ourselves to a view of the universe which, though not rationally demonstrable, is at least reasonable. What our beliefs assert must not, that is to say, conflict with our experience, but should rather aim at making that experience coherent and intelligible. To do so our beliefs must square with the facts of existence as we know them, and, when they go beyond the evidence, must be at least compatible with it. Above all, they must not outrage our intelligence. Judged by these tests, the propositions asserted by the believer in the tenets of the orthodox Christian doctrine, as summarised above, seem to be open to the following objections :

A. They require us to suppose that God is wicked, in which case He cannot be benevolent; or limited, in which case He cannot be omnipotent ; or deceitful, in which case He can be neither benevolent nor omnipotent. This conclusion follows from a consideration of the phenomena of pain and evil.

Two alternatives are here possible : either (i.) God created them or (ii.) He did not.

(i.) Let us first suppose that God deliberately created them. Then we may suppose, further, that they are either (*a*) real or (*b*) in some sense unreal or illusory. If (*a*) they are real, then the deliberate creation of pain and evil is the mark of a wicked person, and God is not benevolent. If (*b*) they are unreal, we must ask how it comes about that we believe them to be real. That we think we suffer, and that we think men do us evil, is undeniable. If these beliefs are false, then, in holding them we are making a mistake. God, aware of the fact that we are making this mis-

take, and knowing, in virtue of His omniscience, that
we should make it, yet deliberately permits us to err.
He is, therefore, responsible for the introduction of
error into the universe. Now, the deliberate creation
of error is as incompatible with the character of a
completely good being as the deliberate creation of
pain and evil. Why, moreover, should God need to
deceive us in the matter, even if we could suppose
that He wished to do so ? Deception springs from
limitation ; we find it necessary to deceive only when
we cannot achieve our ends openly. An all-powerful
being has not the need, an all-good being has not the
wish, to deceive.

(ii.) Let us now suppose that God did not create
pain and evil. Then they must exist independently of
Him, being, on this view, distinct and separate factors or principles in the universe. If God is good, it is
clear that He cannot desire that pain and evil should
exist, and they must exist, therefore, in His despite.
Hence, if God has the wish to remove them and
cannot, it is because He is not all-powerful ; if He has
not the wish, He is not all-good.

These objections to the theory of an omnipotent,
benevolent Creator are sufficiently familiar. As a rule,
no attempt is made to answer them. It is said that the
questions involved are mysteries, which our limited
intelligences are unable to comprehend. We know
that God is good and powerful, and that is enough. If
we do know it, this answer is, of course, satisfactory ;
if not, not. In any event, the resort to faith as a substitute for knowledge, not being based upon rational
grounds, is not susceptible of rational discussion.

Sometimes, however, an attempt is made to reconcile the existence of pain and evil with that of an all-
good God by attributing them to the activities of man.
God, it is said, out of His infinite goodness, bestowed
upon man the gift of free-will. Man has abused this
gift to create evil, and pain is the necessary accom-
paniment of evil. If we ask why man does these

things, the answer is, because of the Fall. But is this
answer satisfactory in the sense required ; does it,
that is to say, absolve God from responsibility ? It is
clear that man could not create pain and evil out of
nothing. They must spring from the innate dispositions and potentialities of his nature. It was because
he was a creature of such a kind that he acted in such
a way. Now, these innate dispositions and potentialities in virtue of which he so acted were implanted in
him by whom ? We can only answer, by man's Creator, who is thus found to be responsible, if not for
the actual introduction of pain and evil into the
world, at least for the creation of beings with the
potentialities from which pain and evil inevitably
sprang. The reply that there was no inevitability
about it, that man was free to do as he chose, and that
the responsibility is therefore man's and not God's,
is evidence of our good intentions towards God, but
is otherwise not convincing. God, being omniscient,
must have known what the result of creating the human race would be. He must, that is to say, have
known that men would utilise their gift of free-will to
introduce pain and evil into the world. Therefore He
deliberately permitted the introduction of pain and
evil into a world that knew them not. In other words,
He deliberately made the experiment of creating the
human race, knowing that evil would come of it. But
this is not the conduct of an all-good being.

B. The orthodox view requires us to suppose that
God's actions are devoid both of point and purpose.
Since God created the world, we must suppose that
there was a time when the world was not ; there was
only God. God *ex hypothesi* is perfect ; therefore, in
the beginning there were absolute goodness and
absolute perfection. How out of this single, all-
embracing goodness pain and evil could be generated, unless the potentiality for their generation was
already present in the goodness—unless, in short, the
goodness was not wholly good—is a difficulty at

which I have already glanced. Let us, however, waive
the question of how and come to the question of why.
That we are imperfect creatures, doing evil and suffering pain, is unfortunately true. But we are assured
that if we behave in the manner which priests en-
join, and of which God approves, our sins will be
forgiven us, and we shall pass beyond this world of
pain and evil into an eternity of bliss.

This process, variously if vaguely described as going
to heaven, being gathered to the bosom of Abraham,
or being made one with God, implies at least this
much, that our imperfections will be shed and that
we shall become perfect. Now, let us suppose that
this consummation is ultimately achieved by all living
creatures, and that the conception of a hell in which
those of us who are unsuccessful in pleasing God
suffer torments throughout eternity is a figment, a
morbid flight of priestly imaginations seeking to re-
venge themselves upon those who have flouted clerical authority. Granting this assumption, we reach the
following position ; suffering and imperfection having
passed away, there remains only the absolute perfection of God and of those who, if still separate from
God (and on this point the Christian religion speaks
with a doubtful voice), are at least perfect, even as
God is perfect. Thus the end of the process is absolute perfection ; but so also was the beginning. The
process, therefore, is circular.

What, then, it may be asked, can be the point of a
journey which, involving pain and evil and imperfection on the way, aims at reaching a goal which is none
other than the starting-point ; or of an undertaking
which, starting from perfection, deliberately gener-
ates pain and evil (or permits them to be generated)
in order that it may achieve perfection ? Assuming
the possibility of such a process, the question of motive seems insoluble.

Finally, it may be asked, why should God create at
all ? He could do so only in so far as He felt the desire,

and desire implies the existence of a need in respect of that which is desired. But a perfect being cannot feel need. For if He be good, His need can only be for that which is good. Hence, God, if He desires, desires something which is good. Now, we cannot desire that which we already possess ; consequently, there must be goods—namely, those which God desires—which He does not already possess. Therefore the sum-total of His goodness could be increased ; therefore He is not as good as possible ; therefore He is not perfect. For these reasons it seems impossible to reconcile the creation of the world by an omnipotent, benevolent Creator with his possession both of omnipotence and of benevolence. These objections apply to the orthodox theological view in so far as it seeks to provide an account of the phenomena of existence.

It seems to me to be further objectionable on moral grounds, as (1) destroying the possibility of ethics and (2) impugning the reality of free-will. Since, moreover, the moral sense and our consciousness of freedom are also facts in the universe which must be accounted for in any comprehensive attempt to explain the world as we find it, we may say that its failure adequately to provide for them constitutes a further objection to the orthodox view in so far as it purports to be true, apart from its deleterious effect upon morality and its discouragement of human effort.

(i.) An omnipotent, benevolent God will do only what is good and will what is good. To do good is, therefore, the same as to do God's will. Once this identification is established, it is impossible to forget it. With the consciousness of God's vigilance ever present to us, we cannot but remember that in doing good we are pleasing God, in doing evil displeasing Him. Now, all religions, as I have already pointed out, have dwelt upon the respective consequences of pleasing and displeasing God with great emphasis, the more advanced religions representing an eternity of absolute bliss as the reward of the one, and of physical torture as the punishment of the other. Thus the injunction to act in accordance with God's will becomes in practice an exhortation not to piety, but to prudence. In practice religion has offered us a choice between two kinds of insurance policy. The one is a short-term insurance policy ; the premiums are negligible and the benefits are reaped in this life ; they are unlimited freedom to gratify our desires and to enjoy what is called a "good time." The other is a long-term policy ; the premiums are paid in the form of self-denial and mortification of the flesh in the present, and the policy is drawn in an eternity of heavenly bliss in the hereafter. Now, directly considerations of this kind are allowed to influence conduct, whether the influence is unconscious or avowed, it is idle to pretend that it is dictated by ethical motives. If we do good because it is God's will, a will of whose power we are only too conscious, and to the dangers of thwarting which we are kept fully alive, it is clear that we do not do good for its own sake ; we do not do it, in other words, because it is good. Yet the possibility of ethics depends upon our ability to prefer good to evil uninfluenced by any other consideration.

(ii.) If God is omniscient, He knows everything ; therefore, He knows the future. He knows, therefore, what is going to happen, and, as He cannot make a mistake, the future is determined because of God's knowledge of it. Therefore we are not free to make the future as we please ; we are not even free to do this or to do that here and now, since, as God knows which of the two we are going to do, our choice between them is already determined.

If the ethical implications of the orthodox view are such as I have indicated, then we shall be averse from embracing it, except under the strongest compulsion from the arguments in its favour. Yet, when assessed in respect of its ability to give a rational account of the universe, it is, as I have tried to show, riddled with contradictions. Judged by the tests suggested above, it does not make our experience intelligible, it does not explain the facts of existence as we know them, it does not square with such evidence as is available, and, so far from satisfying, it offends our intelligence and is repugnant to our moral sense. It seems to follow that, if religion is to be identified with the set of beliefs which I have tried to analyse, it cannot satisfy the conditions indicated at the beginning of the chapter, and it cannot hope to claim the allegiance of the educated mind.

The conclusion is unavoidable ; if the acceptance of this or an equivalent set of beliefs is *all* that we mean by the word religion, then the future must be one without religion. But is it ? Before we can answer we must turn to the second question with which we began this chapter : "How does religion arise, and what is the origin and nature of the need to which it appeals ?" The answer to this question demands a chapter to itself.

Chapter VII

HOW RELIGION AROSE, AND WHY IT FLOURISHED

HOW RELIGION AROSE, AND WHY IT FLOURISHED

An honest God is the noblest work of man.—ANON.

At the end of the last chapter, in discussing the need
for religion, I used the words "origin and nature"
deliberately, because the conjunction of these two
words seems to me to mask a fallacy which it is important to bring to light. The fallacy is to assume
that to lay bare the origins of a thing is tantamount
to describing its present nature.

That this is very far from being the case, I shall try
in the next chapter to show ; yet we more often assume that it is, especially if we are of a scientific turn,
than we are commonly aware, and the assumption is
nowhere more prevalent than in regard to religion.
By most of us, indeed, it is not even realised that an
assumption is involved. We take it for granted that to
demonstrate that religion began as witchcraft, totemism, or exogamy, is to prove that it is in essence no
more than witchcraft, totemism, and exogamy now,
although we should never dream of asserting that the
fact that the savage can only count on the fingers of
one hand, coupled with the demonstration that arith-
metic began with and developed from such counting,
invalidates the multiplication table. To show how a
belief arises is not to describe, still less to discredit it,
and, unless we are to deny to religion the kind of
growth which we are prepared to concede to other
expressions of the human spirit, it is obvious that
there must be more in the religious consciousness
to-day than in the savage fears and flatteries from
which it may be shown to have arisen. And, if there
is, it will be for just that "more" that an account of
religion in terms of its origin and history will fail to
make provision. The point is of importance because
the interpretation of religion in terms of its origin is
often used to prove that religion is not a permanent

and necessary need of the human spirit ; savage in inception, it will, it is urged, disappear when we have finally left our savagery behind us. Religion, it is often said, belongs to the childhood of the race, and will one day be outgrown, together with war and other savage habits, such as the habit of imprisoning men for punishment and animals for show, or the habit of decking the bodies of women with fragments of stone, lumps of metal, and portions of dead birds.

For myself, I do not hold this view, and I shall try in the next chapter to show the fallacy latent in the mode of reasoning upon which it rests. For the present, let us see what the explanations of religions in terms of origin involve.

They are advanced chiefly by anthropologists, who visit remote Melanesian islands for the purpose of observing the religious practices of the natives. Recording them, they conclude that primitive religion is the offspring of human fear and human conceit ; it springs from the desire to propitiate the alien forces of nature, to invest human life with significance in face of the vast indifference of the universe, and to secure the support of an immensely powerful and ferocious personage for the individual, the tribe, or the nation. This general attitude to religion, by ascribing it to a subjective need of human nature, robs it of objective validity. Religion, if this account is correct, is not a revelation of reality, but a symptom of a state of mind ; it is an expression of what man is like. To say that there is God is not to say anything more than that we need to think that there is, and the need is in no sense a guarantee of the existence of that which satisfies it. Thus the great religions of the world are not theology, but psychology ; witnesses, not to the attributes of God, but to the inventive faculty of man. God is not a real being ; He is the image of man, projected, enlarged, upon the empty canvas of the universe.

This view of religion as subjective expresses itself in different forms, according to the nature of the primitive feelings upon which it lays stress. I will take three as examples.

(1) The argument from man's feeling of loneliness and insecurity may be summarised as follows : Human life is immensely insignificant. It is an accidental development of matter, the chance product of forces, an accident unplanned and unforeseen in the history of the planet. A casual and unwanted passenger, it struggles across a fundamentally alien and hostile environment, in which the material and the brutal on all sides condition and determine the spiritual and the vital. One day it will finish its pointless journey with as little noise and significance as, in the person of the amœba, it began it. Until this consummation occurs, man will fare naked and forlorn through an indifferent universe, a puppet twitched into love and war by an indifferent showman who pulls the strings. His destiny is swayed by an inescapable fate ; his fortunes are at the mercy of an irresponsible chance. He is a mere target for the shafts of doom.

These things we know, yet the knowledge is intolerable to us. We cannot bear to be without significance in the universe ; we long to feel that we count, that somehow and to something we matter. And so we invent an immensely powerful and important personage called God, to whom we matter enormously.

By making ourselves important to a person who is Himself so enormously important, we achieve the desired significance, and the more powerful God is conceived to be, the more significant do we, His chief concern, become. So tremendously does He care about us that He has made the material universe for our benefit, this world rightly regarded being merely a school for human nature, in which it is trained and educated for life elsewhere ; while by making Him in our own image we secure His special interest in the human race. The creation of the brute beasts to sustain our bodies and obey our orders is a token of that interest.

Interested as he is in the human species as a whole, he is quite specially interested in the particular race, nation or tribe to which we happen to belong; so that, whatever the quarrel upon which the nation or tribe may happen to be engaged, it may rest assured of his support, since he is guaranteed to take the same view of the rights and wrongs of it as we do ourselves.

Among polytheistic peoples this concept causes no difficulty; each has its own deity or set of deities, and the strongest gods win. But where there is one God, and only one, who sustains the worship and is the repository of the prayers of opposed nations, the zeal of His adherents tends to place the Almighty in a dilemma.

> To God the embattled nations sing and shout,
> "God sträfe England" and "God save the King,"
> God this, God that and God the other thing.
> "Good God!" said God, "I've got my work cut out."

But it is easy to provide for God's solution of the difficulty by invoking His omnipotence.

Interested in the nation or tribe to which we happen to belong, He is quite specially interested in ourselves; interested in and favourable towards, assisting us against those who seek to humiliate us, and generally discomfiting our enemies. This is a world in which the good man is notoriously oppressed, while the wicked flourish like a green bay-tree. The arrangement offends our sense of justice, and, what is more, since we are good men ourselves, it is unfair to us personally. Very well, then, we invent another world in which the good man flourishes eternally and the bad one is eternally punished. Thus the fundamental rightness of things is vindicated, and we incidentally benefit in the process.

But in order that the system may work, it is necessary that the good man and the bad man should be under continual observation, that neither the unrequited goodness of the one nor the unchastised

badness of the other may go unregistered. This function is admirably performed by the vertical or up-
stairs God. Thoughtfully accommodated with an
abode in the skies, a position admirably adapted for
purposes of espionage, He keeps a dossier of each
individual, recognising in us the worth that others
unaccountably fail to recognise, and observing the
wickedness and hypocrisy of those whom the world
equally unaccountably exalts. These things are carefully noted, and in the next world all is made right.
Immensely important, admired and envied—for are
we not the favoured children of Omnipotence ?—we
live happily ever afterwards ; scorned and hated, our
enemies are convincingly humiliated. Assuredly an
admirable arrangement ! It is difficult to see how it
could be improved upon. But God is essential to its
proper working, and God flourishes accordingly.

God, then, on this view, is at once the product of
human terror and the prop of human pride. He com-
forts our wretchedness, calms our fears, gives us an
assurance of justice, and makes us feel important.
"Religious ideas," says Freud, "have sprung from
the same need as all the other achievements of culture ; from the necessity for defending oneself against
the crushing supremacy of nature."

(2) But though Freud recognises one of the sources
of religion in man's subjection to the forces of nature,
he finds its chief root in his relationship to society.
Hence his main account of the origin of religion is
rather different from that just summarised.

This account will be found in Freud's book, *The
Future of an Illusion*, which appeared in 1928. It is
not very original, but it is typical of a certain attitude
to religion, and may be taken as fairly representative
of the view of many educated people, especially psychological and scientific workers to-day. Freud proceeds upon the basis of what is, in effect, a social
contract theory of the origin of society. This theory
is admirably stated early in the second book of Plato's

Republic. Essential to it is the conception of primitive man as a completely non-moral animal ; as such his natural inclination is to get his own way at all costs, without thought of the consequences to his neighbours. If his neighbour annoys him, he knocks him on the head ; if his neighbour's wife attracts him, he makes off with her. Thus every man has, as Glaucon puts it in the *Republic*, a *natural* tendency to do injustice to his fellows. Admirable in theory, this system, or lack of system, has one serious drawback in practice ; the right of every man to do injustice to his neighbours carries with it a corresponding right on the part of his neighbours to do injustice to him. He is one, but his neighbours are many, with the result that, where his hand is against every man and every man's hand is against him, he tends to get the worst of the bargain. His existence is intolerably insecure, he must be perpetually on his guard, and he has no secure enjoyment of his possessions. In the days before society was formed man's life, as the philosopher Hobbes puts it, was "nasty, brutish, and short." Finding the situation intolerable, men ended it by making a compact known as the social contract.

The compact was to form society. Consenting to live in society, man surrendered his natural right to do what he pleased to his fellows, on condition that they made a similar concession as regards himself. Social relations were regulated by public opinion, which later crystallised into law, and man for the future restrained his natural instincts lest he incur the social displeasure of his fellows. Thus was society formed, and from its formation springs the system of inhibitions and restraints which men call morality. To act morally is thus, as we have seen in chapter iv.,[1] the reverse of acting naturally and implies a victory over the "natural man" ; we obey the law, and keep our hands off our neighbour's wife and property, not because we are by nature moral, but in fear of the penal-

[1] See pp. 62, 63.

ties with which society has proscribed actions which violate the contract upon which it was formed. In other words, we do right only through fear of the consequences of doing wrong. Remove this fear of consequences, as, for example, by endowing the individual with the gift of invisibility at will, and the social man would immediately relapse into the natural man, with the result that no property would be safe, no wife inviolable. The conclusion is that morality, which is simply the habit of acting in a manner of which other people approve, is not natural to man ; on the contrary, it runs counter to his natural interests, frustrates his natural desires, and requires him to surrender his natural rights.

Now, man is not born social. He only becomes so at the cost of suffering and repression. Every child is born "natural," endowed with an egotism that bids him tyrannise over his world. Seeking to impose his imperious will upon his environment, he is surprised when his environment fails to respond, pained when it begins to resent. For a creature who starts with this "natural" endowment the business of growing up into a social adult who knows the lawful limits that must be set upon his desires is, it is obvious, a formidable one, so formidable that, according to Freud, it is seldom more than partially achieved, and never achieved without suffering and injury. To assist him in the difficult process of social adjustment the individual invokes the aid of religion. Hence the essence of religion, according to Freud, is compensation. It is compensation for man's loneliness in face of the vast indifference of the universe ; it is also, and more importantly, compensation for the renunciations which he must undertake at the bidding of society.

Wherein [asks Freud] lies the peculiar virtue of religious ideas ? We have spoken of the hostility to culture produced by the pressure it exercises and the instinctual renunciations that it demands. If one imagined its prohibitions removed, then one could choose any woman who took one's fancy as one's sexual object, one

HR

could kill without hesitation one's rival or whoever interfered
with one in any other way, and one could seize what one
wanted of another man's goods without asking his leave : how
splendid, what a succession of delights life would be !

Forgo these delights, we must, if we are to achieve
civilisation. And, forgoing them, we demand that
the gods shall reward us for our sacrifice. Hence
religion is the force that reconciles man to the burden
of civilisation. It is the most important of the compensations that civilisation offers to its citizens ; so important that only by offering it does civilisation become possible. When we have learned as by second
nature to refrain from incest, murder, torture, and
arson, when we "pass right along the car, please,"
adjust our dress before leaving, and take our places at
the end of the queue, without thinking whether we
want to do these things or not, the external restric-
tions which society imposes have become instinctive
habits, the primitive child has become the civilised
adult, and social adjustment has been achieved. But
achieved only by the aid of religion. Had we no God
to whom to turn for comfort and consolation, to
whom to tell the unfulfilled wishes and thwarted
ambitions, to whom to pray for fortitude to suffer and
strength to forbear, the task would be too great for us.
With the very dawn of consciousness, the need for a
father confessor makes itself felt.

Thus little by little I became conscious where I was, and to
have a wish to express my wishes to those who could content
them ; and I could not ; for the wishes were within me and they
without ; nor could they, by any sense of theirs, enter within my
spirit.

Thus St. Augustine, who proceeds to tell how he
sought and found in God the confidant whom the
world denied.

Nor is it only from others that we need a refuge.
There is the riot of our desires, there are the prickings

of our consciences ; there is the sting of remorse. For, though manhood is achieved, the adjustment to society is not yet complete ; still, though with de- creasing vigour as the individual grows older and society more civilised, the natural man raises his head and rebels. When the rebellion comes into the open, when we refuse to pass down the car, take the head of the queue, or insist upon our inalienable privilege of driving upon the right-hand side of the road, society has little difficulty in quelling us. There are police- men, there are law courts, there are prisons, there are even scaffolds. But sometimes the rebellion stays un- derground, or, though it comes to the surface, goes undetected.

Against these hidden revolts society must protect itself, and evolves accordingly a system of espionage. There is a spy within the individual citadel itself, a spy in the service of society. This is our old Victor- ian acquaintance, the conscience, the policeman of society, stationed within the individual to see that social interests are duly observed. Directly we go wrong, directly, that is to say, we cease to act in a way of which society approves, conscience begins to nag. Like a dog that does not stop us from passing, but that we cannot prevent from barking, conscience voices the disapproval of society. The voice of con- science is an unpleasant one, causing us grave dis- comfort, and in extreme cases driving us to madness. Some refuge from the stings of conscience we must find, and we duly find it—in religion. Stricken by re- morse, we demand that our sins be forgiven us. Who can forgive sin but God ? Fouled by our sins of wrong-doing, we demand to be made clean. How can we be cleansed save by bathing in the blood of Jesus ? And so we come to a new function of religion, a new use for God. Again religion takes the form of an in- surance. We deny ourselves the minor luxuries, ab- stain from the grosser forms of vice, and submit to a little boredom on Sunday, and in return we are guaranteed against discomfort from the stings of conscience in the present and possible discomfort at the hands of the Almighty in the hereafter.

In all these ways and in many others religion seeks to compensate us for the strain and stress of living in society.

Freud traces the gradual evolution of religion to perform this function and the success with which it has, in fact, performed it. He distinguishes various stages in the growth of religion, determined by the nature of the need which at each successive stage it has been chiefly invoked to satisfy. Initially, the chief use of the gods is to protect man from the capriciousness of nature ; but, as man progressed, the discoveries of science introduced order into disorder, and substituted law for caprice. At the same time, the growing complexity of civilisation increases the strain of social adjustment. Less needed in the physical world, God becomes an indispensable refuge for the harassed soul of man. Thus history records a decline in the physical and a growth in the moral attributes of the gods.

In the course of time the first observations of law and order in natural phenomena are made, and therewith the forces of nature lose their human traits. But men's helplessness remains, and with it their father-longing and the gods. . . . And the more autonomous nature becomes and the more the gods withdraw from her, the more earnestly are all expectations concentrated on the third task assigned to them and the more does morality become their real domain. It now becomes the business of the gods to adjust the defects and evils of culture, to attend to the sufferings that men inflict on each other in their communal life, and to see that the laws of culture, which men obey so ill, are carried out. The laws of culture themselves are claimed to be of divine origin, they are elevated to a position above human society, and they are extended over nature and the universe.

Thus Freud records the progress of religion, and summarises the different functions which it performs. Nor is his account singular. On the contrary, it is one to which, with minor modifications, most psychologists and anthropologists would subscribe. The more we learn about our mental, the more we learn about our bodily natures, the more, it is said, do we lay bare the roots of religion in the fundamental needs of our natures. Psychologists derive the doctrine of original sin from the sense of man's impotence in the face of chance and destiny, physiologists from the transgressions of his passionate body against the taboos of society. From our infancy we walk between a fear and a fear, between ruthless Nature and restricting culture, crying, like Bunyan's Pilgrim, "What shall I do to be saved?" And, demanding salvation at all costs, we create God to save us.

Thus religion is the consolation of mankind, and as such its appeal is universal.

(3) But we now come to a more limited, but scarcely less important, function which religion has played in the history of man. To its successful performance of this function its growth and vigour in more modern times is mainly attributable.

There are evils which are the common heritage of all men ; they are death, disease, the ingratitude of man to man, the malevolence of destiny. These are no respecters of persons, and bear with impartial severity upon us all. But there are others which do not belong to the essential conditions of human life, but are incidental to the way in which man has chosen collectively to organise his life. For men, equal in the eyes of God, are far from equal in the eyes of society. There are, and always have been, rulers and ruled, oppressors and oppressed, rich and poor ; according to many authorities, there always will be. Society, moreover, is based upon force, which its rulers employ to maintain and perpetuate the inequalities on which they thrive. To make their task easier they invoke the assistance of religion. For religion is not only a means of reconciling the individual to society ; it is also, and more particularly, a device for inducing the poor and oppressed to tolerate the particular

order of society which impoverishes and oppresses
them. Thus religion becomes the instrument of the
rich and the bridle of the poor. How is the oracle
worked ?

It is significant, in the first place, that most religions
extol the virtues appropriate to slaves—namely,
meekness, humility, unselfishness, and contentment,
and censure as the vices of pride and presumption
the virtues of courage, originality, and independence,
and that passionate resentment at injustice and wrong
which are characteristic of those who aspire to rise
above their servitude. The Christian religion goes
further, and makes a virtue of poverty. It is only, we
are assured, with the greatest difficulty that the rich
man shall enter the Kingdom of Heaven, which opens
its gates to the humble and needy. Poverty and insignificance are not, therefore, as they appear to be,
and as the world insists on regarding them, disabili-
ties to be avoided at all costs ; they are passports to
celestial bliss. As such they are rightly to be wel-
comed. The Christian religion, indeed, expressly
encourages us to cultivate them, exhorting us to
worldly improvidence and inertia by bidding us take
no thought for the morrow and to be content with
that state of life into which it has pleased God to
call us.

As it has pleased Him to call ninety-nine out of
every hundred of us to an extremely lowly state,
religion, in so far as it is taken seriously, assists in
keeping us where we are. Assists whom ? Those who
benefit by our remaining where we are—namely, our
rulers. For the governing classes have been quick to
seize the chance religion has offered them of not only
subduing their inferiors, but of representing their
subjection as a positive asset to their subjects. Ever
since an early governing-class realist slipped the par-
able about Lazarus into the text of the Gospel of
St. Luke, the priest and the parson, seeking to persuade the poor that it was only by remaining poor

that they would go to heaven, have been able to produce good scriptural backing for their propaganda.
The poor, on the whole, have been only too ready to
agree, and have gladly embraced the promise of celestial bliss in the next world as a compensation for the
champagne and cigars they were missing in this one.
Since the celestial bliss was known to be of indefinite
continuance, while the champagne and cigars could
not last at most for more than a beggarly fifty years
(as a matter of fact, they often lasted less, God having
from time to time seen fit to punish the excesses of
the worldly by dulling their palates and depriving
them of their appetites in the present as an earnest of
His intentions for the future[1]), the poor—it is obvious
—have the best of the bargain. If it has ever occurred
to them to wonder why the rich and powerful should
recklessly jeopardise the chances which they have so
freely proffered and warmly recommended to their
poorer brethren, they may possibly have comforted
themselves with the reflection that *quem deus vult
perdere prius dementit*. Possibly, but not probably,
for, on the whole, the poor and oppressed have been
too much engaged with their poverty and oppression
to reflect upon the motives of their betters.

Religion, from this point of view, is a gigantic social
hoax, a hoax which has been, on the whole, remark-
ably successful, so much so, indeed, that from time
to time one or another of the rulers of mankind,
franker or more secure than the rest, has not scrupled
to show how the trick was worked. Thus Napoléon,
a notorious sceptic, taxed with the protection which
he afforded to a religion in which he did not believe,
and stoutly refusing to be drawn into anti-Christian
or anti-clerical legislation :

"What is it," he asked his critics, "that makes the poor man think
it quite natural that there are fires in my palace while he is dying

---

[1] More recently, of course, He has added cancer to the list of
penalties.

of cold ? that I have ten coats in my wardrobe while he goes
naked ? that at each of my meals enough is served to feed his
family for a week ? It is simply religion, which tells him that in
another life I shall be only his equal, and that he actually has more
chance of being happy there than I. Yes, we must see to it that the
floors of the churches are open to all, and that it does not cost the
poor man much to have prayers said on his tomb."

Napoléon was right. The poor have a need for religion which the rich do not feel, and it is not surprising,
therefore, to find that, while scepticism and atheism
have on occasion flourished among the rich, religion
has uniformly been embraced with eagerness by the
poor. The growth of disbelief in governing-class
circles, while it may have evoked the censure of
society—the rich have always thought it prudent to
keep up religious observances—has rarely called down
the penalties of the law. Thus governing-class writers
of the eighteenth century, Gibbon, Voltaire, or the
Encyclopædists, for example, who were notoriously
irreligious or hostile to religion, went comparatively
scatheless. Naturally, since they wrote for the educated upper, not for the ignorant lower, classes. Most
of the early rationalists, again, were academic people
whose books were too difficult or too dull to command a popular circulation. Excepting Woolston,
they escaped unpunished. But Peter Annett, a school-
master who tried to popularise free thought and held
forth on the village green, was sentenced to the pil-
lory and hard labour in 1763. "If we take the cases in
which the civil authorities have intervened to repress
the publication of unorthodox opinions during the
last two centuries," says Professor Bury, "we find
that the object has always been to prevent the spread
of free thought among the masses."[1]
On the whole, however, the governing classes have
thought it wiser themselves to profess allegiance to
the religion which they cultivated for the benefit of
others. Nor has the profession been always insincere.

[1] Bury, *A History of Freedom of Thought*, p. 222.

Using religion as an instrument, they have nevertheless revered it.

In the nineteenth century, as the danger to society from the new proletariat first made itself felt, the beliefs of the governing classes, it is interesting to note, become more pronounced as their religious example becomes more edifying. It was most important that the wage slaves of the industrial revolution should learn to know God, and in knowing Him to respect their betters. Their betters, then, should show them the way. This they proceeded to do.

The *Annual Register* for 1798 remarks :

> It was a wonder to the lower orders throughout all parts of England to see the avenues to the churches filled with carriages. This novel appearance prompted the simple country people to enquire what was the matter.

Soon afterwards Wilberforce managed to get the first day of meeting of the House of Commons put off to Tuesday, lest the re-assembling of Parliament on a Monday might cause members to travel and to be seen travelling through London on a Sunday. For the same reason the opening of the Newmarket Races was changed from Easter Monday to Tuesday. "In the old times the villages on the route used to turn out on Easter Sunday to admire the procession of rich revellers, and their gay colours and equipment. The Duke of York, in answer to remonstrances, said that it was true he travelled to the races on a Sunday, but he always had a Bible and a Prayer Book in his carriage."

The moral of all this is sufficiently obvious. It was, indeed, put succinctly enough by one Arthur Young, who, in *An Enquiry into the State of Mind Among the Lower Classes*, written in 1798, says :

> A stranger would think our churches were built, as indeed they are, only for the rich. Under such arrangement where are the lower classes to hear the Word of God, that Gospel which in our Saviour's time was preached more particularly to the poor ?

Where are they to learn the doctrines of that truly excellent religion which exhorts to content and to submission to the higher
powers ? . . .

Twenty years later, one Englishman out of seven being at that
time a pauper, Parliament voted a million of public money for
the construction of churches to preach submission to the higher
powers. In the debates in the House of Lords, in May 1818,
Lord Liverpool laid stress on the social importance of guiding
by this means the opinions of those who were beginning to
receive education.[1]

That the position remains radically unaltered is
shown by the following dialogue between Cusins and
Undershaft from Shaw's *Major Barbara*, a dialogue
which has become a classic.

Cusins (in a white fury) : Do I understand you to imply that you
can buy Barbara ?
Undershaft : No ; but I can buy the Salvation Army.
Cusins : Quite impossible.
Undershaft : You shall see. All religious organisations exist by
selling themselves to the rich.
Cusins : Not the Army. That is the Church of the poor.
Undershaft : All the more reason for buying it.
Cusins : I don't think you quite know what the Army does for the
poor.
Undershaft : Oh yes, I do. It draws their teeth: that is enough for
me—as a man of business——
Cusins : Nonsense ! It makes them sober——
Undershaft : I prefer sober workmen. The profits are larger.
Cusins : —honest——
Undershaft : Honest workmen are the most economical.
Cusins : —attached to their homes——
Undershaft : So much the better : they will put up with anything
sooner than change their shop.
Cusins : —happy——
Undershaft : An invaluable safeguard against revolution.
Cusins : —unselfish——
Undershaft : Indifferent to their own interests, which suits me
exactly.
Cusins : —with their thoughts on heavenly things——
Undershaft (rising) : And not on Trade Unionism nor Socialism.
Excellent.
Cusins (revolted) : You really are an infernal old rascal.

[1] J. L. and Barbara Hammond, *The Town Labourer*, 1760–1832,
pp. 234, 235.

Summing up, we may note that this conception of the special function of religion as the instrument of the rich and the bridle of the poor follows logically from its main social function considered above. I have already summarised Freud's account of religion as man's compensation for the renunciations which society demands of him. This may be described as the general social function of religion. It is the part which religion has been called upon to play in the lives of tribal and civilised men, because they live in tribes and societies. But in addition to the general there is a special social function of religion, which is to render the inequalities of society tolerable to the masses. Civilisation, requiring of the many poor far greater instinctive renunciations than it demands of the rich, has given them far fewer material compensations. It is essential, therefore, if they are to acquiesce in a state of society which on the material side demands so much while giving so little, that they should receive some compensation of the spirit, a compensation which brings comfort in the present and gives hope for the future. Such compensation is afforded by an ingeniously devised and richly satisfying religious system, which, while making a virtue of humility, feeds the fires of self-esteem, lest, revolting against their insignificance, the poor and the many should turn against society and destroy it. This, then, is one of the functions which religion, and especially the Christian religion, has performed in civilised societies ; it has taken the revolutionary sting from poverty and blunted the edge of present discontent with promises of future well-being. Performing this function, religion has been sedulously exploited and used by the rich as an instrument of class domination. God, it has been found, is cheaper than a living wage. Very well, then, let us invest in Him ! Religion is a show to keep the poor amused. Very well, then, let us build churches in the slums ! For this reason Socialists have tended to be hostile to religion, and the Bol-

shevik Government veers between reluctant toleration and covert persecution.

In this chapter I have endeavoured briefly to summarise a number of different accounts of the origin,
the growth, and the function of religion. These accounts dominate the modern psychological and socio-
logical treatment of the subject, which is, on the whole,
markedly hostile to religion. There are, admittedly,
differences on points of detail and different writers put
the emphasis differently according to the purposes
which their account is intended to serve and the aspect of religion with which it is chiefly concerned.
But all the accounts which I have summarised are in
fundamental agreement in interpreting religion on
subjectivist lines.

On this one fundamental point they concur. When
faced with the question, "Why is there religion ? "
they answer unanimously, "Because man wants it."
When asked, "Whence does religion rise ? " their
reply is, "From the needs of man's nature." Pressed
for an explanation of its authority and appeal, they
represent it as a "rationalisation of his instinctive
wishes." Thus all these accounts are in their different
ways subjectivist. They affirm that religion enables
man to accommodate himself to this world, that it
expresses a human need, and that it is, therefore,
pleasant and consoling ; they do not say that it repre-
sents an objective fact, that it points forward to a
different world, and that it is therefore true. With
most of what they assert I am largely, if not entirely,
in agreement. I think that the interpretations they
give of the origin of religion in terms of the needs
which it fulfils, and of the ground of its appeal in
terms of the wishes that it rationalises, are in the
main true. But I do not think that they are complete.
They are, that is to say, interpretations in terms of
origin only, and they take no account of the conception of end or purpose. They ask how religion began
and why it flourished ; they do not ask what it may

become. Both conceptions are, I am convinced, necessary to an adequate description of the status of religion in the present, and a reasoned estimate of its chance of survival in the future.

In the next chapter, then, I shall consider the reasons for including in our survey an account of religion in terms of what it may become.

Chapter VIII

THE EVOLUTION OF RELIGION

Chapter VIII

THE EVOLUTION OF RELIGION

The nature of man is not what he is born as, but what he is born for.—ARISTOTLE.

I

To the modern criticism of religion which I briefly outlined in the last chapter, there is one very obvious retort. It takes the form of what is vulgarly known as a *tu quoque*. If it can be shown, as the critics of religion allege, that our beliefs are the projections of our wishes, why is it only to our religious beliefs that the demonstration applies ? People who have believed in the existence of God have admittedly wished to believe in the existence of God. Very well, then, so runs the criticism, their belief reflects nothing but their wish ; it does not mean that there is a God. But has nobody ever wished to discredit religion ? Obviously they have. Very well, then, the belief that religion is merely the reflection of a subjective need and therefore false, reflects nothing but the wish to find it so. It does not mean that religion *is* merely the reflection of a subjective need and *is* therefore false. If the point were purely a logical one, I should not press it. To score logical points against an opponent is apt to irritate one's reader, especially if he is an English reader, as much as one's opponent, and the prudent controversialist will refrain. But the point is more than a logical one.

Modern psychologists, especially modern psychoanalysts, are continually deriding religious beliefs on the ground that they spring from tainted motives. Because of these motives, they hold, the believer is predisposed to find the evidence in favour of the belief he professes ; when the evidence is doubtful, he cooks it ; when it is wanting altogether, he invents it. That the religious apologist does, in fact, do these things is not doubted. The Christian treatment of evi-

IR

dence in connection with the argument from design to which I referred in chapter iii.,[1] is a startling witness to the dishonesty of the human mind when it is constrained by the necessity of arriving at a foregone conclusion.

But is the reasoning of religious apologists alone suspect ? I doubt it. Modern psychologists, especially modern psycho-analysts, often argue as if, while everybody else's intellectual motives were tainted, they alone are animated by the single and simple desire to discover the truth. It never seems to occur to them that the desire to discredit religion may be as strong as the desire to believe in it; the motives for thinking it false as strong as those for thinking it true. And, if they are as strong, then, according to the doctrine which we are asked to accept, the arguments of the critics of religion will own as subjective a basis, will be the projections of as strong a set of wishes, reflections of as marked a bias, as those of its upholders. And not only the arguments, but also the evidence. For, if the Christian apologist cooks the evidence to feed his preconceived desire, so may the Christian critic. Indeed, if the psycho-analyst is right, he must do so ; and we have only to read the literature of psychoanalysis on the subject to realise that he does.

Religion, Freud concludes, is derivable in part from the Œdipus complex. So, incidentally, are most of the other manifestations of the human spirit. The conclusion once announced, the evidence is subjected to the most intolerable strain to support it. Freud, indeed, is as anxious to believe in the importance of sex in early life as a saint is anxious to believe in the importance of God in after-life, and, while exposing the unconscious bias that inspires the arguments of theologians, he overlooks the influence of the reverse bias on his own.

Religious mysticism, Professor Leuba concludes, is in the main a rationalisation of frustrated sexual de-

[1] See pp. 42, 43.

sires. The virgin mystics, needing a man, have found God. Professor Leuba has written a large and carefully documented work called *The Psychology of Religious Mysticism* to illustrate and enforce his thesis. Yet great as must be the admiration of every reader for the patience and thoroughness with which Professor Leuba has collected, and the clarity and scholarship with which he has collated the material of his book, he cannot avoid the suspicion that certain predominant interests have governed the author's labours, determining both his selection of the evidence and his interpretation of the evidence selected. He sets out to show that mysticism reflects the physiological and/or psychological condition of the mystic, and, on the whole, his book shows it, but, in showing it, shows also that the author wanted to show it, and is diminished in respect of its trustworthiness accordingly.

Such instances could be multiplied a hundredfold. Again and again the critics of religion are seen to be guilty of the same process of rationalisation in the interests of their unconscious wishes as that which they detect and criticise in its apologists; inevitably, if they are right, since our reasons, being evolved to enable us to invent arguments for what we instinctively want to do and justifications for what we instinctively want to believe, must needs fulfil the function assigned to them. In doing so our reasons deceive us as to the nature of the thing reasoned about; they represent it as we should like it to be rather than as it is, and they are capable, if put to it, of inventing it or abolishing it altogether.

I cannot myself subscribe to this conception of reason. To me it seems that reasoning may, and often does, provided of course that we reason well enough, give us truth, truth, that is to say, not about ourselves, but about something outside ourselves. We think, for example, that three and two make five, not because we want to think it, but because they do make five ; that the constituents of water are H_2O, not because this particular combination satisfies some atavistic need, but because they are; that the whole is greater than the part, because it is; and that A cannot both be A and not A, because it cannot. Taking this view that reason is sometimes unbiassed, and that, when it is so, it may give us truth, I do not press this criticism of the psychologists and psycho-analysts, which is valid only if we accept *their* account of the function of reason. I merely point out that, if we accept it, then it operates against its exponents as effectively as against the believers in and apologists for religion, and that, while it is employed to demonstrate that religion is false because it is merely a rationalisation of the wishes of those who believe in it, it invalidates the demonstration for precisely the same reason —namely, because it is a rationalisation of the wishes of those who employ it. In other words, the modern criticism of religion, in so far as it proves its point, stultifies itself, and in stultifying itself disproves its point. If we refuse to accept it, at any rate in its entirety, then we are no longer required to dismiss religion as a mere rationalisation. It may be so, of course, but it is not necessarily so. We can, therefore, proceed to consider the case for religion on merits.

II

And here I wish to take up the thread of certain observations which I made in the last chapter with regard to the various alternative types of explanation which may be adopted by those seeking to give an account of a thing, with particular reference to that type of explanation which interprets the present state of a thing in terms of its origin.

Now, all the accounts of religion summarised in chapter vi. define and explain it in terms of its earliest beginnings in human fear and need. Accepting these accounts in the main as far as they went,

they were not, I urged, necessarily complete. Why
not ? Because to explain a thing in terms of its origin
is not to give a complete account of it as it is now.
For a complete account we must consider not only its
origin, but its consummation ; we must, in other
words, not only look backwards to the germ from
which it arose, but forwards to the end which it is
seeking to achieve. The present state of a growing and
developing thing reflects its past, no doubt ; but it
also foreshadows its future.

Suppose, for example, we take as an example of
such a growing and developing thing a youth of fif-
teen years old. How are we to describe his nature ?
To know that he was once an embryo, and that his
body still bears the traces of having been a fish is no
doubt important ; but it is equally, perhaps more,
important to know that he will one day be a man. We
may go further and say that it is only in so far as he
does one day become a man that he realises his full
nature and becomes fully himself. In so far as he falls
short of manhood, in so far as his faculties are still
immature and his body undeveloped, he has not attained the proper form of his species, and has not,
therefore, realised all that he has it in him to be. The
nature of a growing thing, in other words, is not
exhibited at some half-way-house stage on the road
to its full development ; it is exhibited at, because it
is only realised at, its full development. To give a
complete account of it, therefore, we must await that
development.

The moral is that, if you want to know the nature
of a man, you must take him in the full flood of his
energies and exercise of his powers ; you must take
him, in fact, at his zenith. Until he reaches it, he is
not yet completely himself, he is only trying to become himself. And since, while his nature falls short
of its full development, he is only incompletely himself, it follows that your description of his nature, as
it is in his immaturity, will be only incompletely a

description. To make it complete you must include a reference to what he is trying to become.

Or take an institution in which there is organised a number of people living a common way of life, inspired by a common purpose, and owning common loyalties; take, for example, a State. States as we know them are imperfect and incomplete; they are founded on inequality and maintained by injustice, and their governors seek to perpetuate the anomalies on which they thrive. Moreover, though democratic in form, the modern Western community is far from being democratic in fact, and the system of representative government, which professes to ascertain and to embody the will of the people through the machinery of the ballot box, is little more than an elaborate device for giving the appearance and withholding the reality. These things are commonplaces; we all know them, and because of them we say that States are imperfect and incomplete. We also know how the modern State arose, and trace its origin in the tribal institutions of primitive societies. What are we to say of these institutions? Manifestly that, considered as States, they are still more imperfect, still more incomplete. The dreams of philosophers, not the records of historians, place the ideal State in man's remote past.

Now let us suppose that we were to give an account of the State as it is to-day solely in terms of its past history, and, describing the tribal origins from which it has arisen, were to interpret its institutions solely in the light of those origins. Our account, it is obvious, would be grossly misleading. It would omit all those characteristics in virtue of which the modern State has developed beyond its early prototypes, and in the course of its development has become a less incomplete approximation to what a State should be, a less imperfect realisation of the State's true nature. So far, then, our account would be incomplete. How are we to complete it? In the first place, by including those features in respect of which a complex modern society differs from a primitive tribal one. So much is obvious. But not only these, for our account, to be adequate, must make acknowledgement not only to the State's past, but to its future—not only to what it has been, but to what it is trying to become. For, in so far as it still falls short of its full development, the modern State is to that extent not completely a State, just as a youth in his teens is not completely a man, and an account of the nature of the State based on a description of the States as they are would, therefore, not be a complete account. To determine what the true nature of the State is, we must, it is clear, look not merely to its elementary beginnings, not merely to its present immaturity, but to the condition of perfected development which it may one day achieve. And just as we may say of a youth that he is trying to become a man, and that, until he does so, he has not completely realised his nature, so we may say of all the imperfect States in which men have hitherto been organised that they too are trying to realise more completely their full nature as States. Until they do so, they are not fully themselves.

What is the moral ? That to understand the nature of a thing you must look not merely to its beginnings, not even to the present stage of development which it may have happened to achieve, but to its fully developed condition. Until that condition is realised, its nature is not fully revealed.

If a thing's nature is exhibited only in its complete development, a complete account of its nature can be given only in terms of that development. Thus, to describe its nature *as it is now*, we must seek to estimate its future ; so only can we hope to understand the tentative beginnings and premonitory stirrings that foreshadow it. A thing reflects its past, no doubt, and to understand it we must know its past ; but it also foreshadows its future, and to understand it we must seek to forecast its future ; and we must do this

not only as a disinterested exercise in prophecy, but
because the future in part determines and renders
intelligible the present. It follows that adequately to
understand a growing and developing thing we must
take into account not only the origins from which it
sprang, but the goal which it may be seeking to
achieve. We must think of it not only as determined
from behind by its past, but determined from in
front by its future. We must, in a word, introduce the
notion of purpose.

Our conclusion is in accordance with, indeed it
is demanded by, the teaching of evolution. Life,
we are agreed, changes ; it evolves. If the changes
which evolution implies are real changes—and
if they are not, everything that exists must have
existed always, and time and growth and movement
are illusions—then at any given stage in the growth
of a living organism the organism must be different
from what it was at the preceding stages. But it not
only changes ; it develops, and in saying that it develops we are implying that at each stage it is not only
different from but also more than it was before. Consider, for example, the case of the growing human
body. The matter of which a living body is composed, beginning as a microscopic speck of proto-
plasm, ends as a many-millioned colony of cells.
These cells are highly organised, and specialised for
the performance of different functions. Some are
marshalled to carry on the work of the nervous
system ; others to form the engines we call muscles ;
others, again, serve the comparatively lowly purpose
of bone-levers. Instruments of incredible delicacy,
the eye and the ear, are evolved ; yet the whole complex mechanism of a living human body is developed
from a particle of living matter smaller than the finest
pin-head. Now, either these complex cells and organs
were present in the pin-head to begin with, or they
were not. If they were not, then they are literally new ;
there was, that is to say, a time when they were not,

and we are entitled to say that there is more in the present state of the body than there was in its origin.

What is true of the life of the body is true also of that of the mind. Knowledge which is literally new comes into the world. An engineer knows how to build a bridge, a mathematician understands the differential calculus. Either this knowledge and this understanding are new in the sense that there was a time when no mind possessed them, or they are not. If they are not, then they existed in some form when the earth was populated by amœbas. A similar argument may be applied to any other planet upon which life has appeared, the conclusion being that there is nothing new under the sun. Thus change is unreal, since whatever is always has been, and evolution is an illusion. If they are new, then there was a time when the universe knew them not ; in other words, they have appeared from nowhere, since there is nowhere outside the universe, and evolved out of nothing. Granted, then, that the fact of growth implies the coming into being of new elements, that there may be more in a thing's present state than there was in its ingredients or its origin, granted further that this is true of the human mind or spirit, why should we deny its application to the expressions of the human spirit, to art, for example, to science or to religion ? To art and to science, indeed, we apply it readily enough ; but what of religion ? Why should we arbitrarily exclude religion from the operation of the laws of growth and development ? For it is high time to apply these considerations to the subject of this book. Applying them, we assert that religion can no more receive an adequate interpretation in terms of its origin alone than can any other growing and developing thing. This is not to say that the interpretation in terms of origin is inappropriate, but merely that it is not complete ; it is not complete because the religious consciousness is more than the ingredients from which it has emerged.

It is also more than the psychological machinery which is involved in its emergence. Psycho-analysts are fond of pointing out that religion is sublimated emotion. Primitive lusts, social maladjustments and misfits and unacknowledged desires are mixed together in an unholy brew of which the religious consciousness is the distilled essence. The ingredients exposed, it is somehow implied that their outcome is discredited. Erroneously, for to lay bare the assorted and possibly disreputable elements of which the religious consciousness may have been compounded is not to show that they *are* that consciousness ; the theory of sublimation, if it means anything at all, means, in fact, that they are not.

A chocolate from a slot machine is the outcome of a series of complex chemical ingredients and mechanical processes. If I were to take the trouble, I could find out what the processes are which go to the production of the chocolate and the ingredients of which it is compounded. I could even describe them in a book. But I should not imagine, nor would my readers imagine, that I was describing the chocolate, still less that, by cataloguing its ingredients and demonstrating the processes from which it had resulted, I had in some mysterious way explained away the chocolate. You cannot, admittedly, have the chocolate without the ingredients and the mechanism. But it does not follow that the ingredients and the mechanism are identical with their product. This fact recognised in the kitchen and the factory is overlooked in the study and the consulting-room. Refusing to overlook it, I assert that an account of the origin, the history and the psychology of religion, interesting as it is to the anthropologist, the historian, and the psychologist, is not an account of religion, and that arguments derived from it cannot, therefore, be used to discredit or to dispose of religion. Were it not for the fears of the savage and the social maladjustments of the citizen, religion admittedly would be very different from what it is. But, originating in the stress of human need and flowering on the dunghill of human emotions, the religious consciousness rises above its origins and transcends its machinery. The mechanism, I repeat, is other than its product.

In its account of religion, and not of religion alone, psycho-analysis makes the mistake of identifying, and therefore confusing, the unconscious trends of our nature with their conscious outcrop. Unmasking the malevolence of our unconscious wishes, analysts exhibit the ingenuity with which they are sublimated to appear honourable ; they succeed ; but they also exhibit the efficiency with which they are sublimated so that they are indeed honourable. One day, no doubt, psycho-analysts will succeed, if they have not done so already, in reducing the sense of duty to something else, probably to something discreditable, but this would not explain away the sense of duty any more than the successful reduction of matter to electricity explains away matter, or of religion to the needs and desires of which it can be shown to be a sublimation explains away religion.

For this reason, criticisms of religion urged by psycho-analysts, valid up to a point, are valueless beyond it. It is not that they are not true, but that they are incomplete.

If religion does, in fact, derive from the sources summarised in the last chapter, if it has fulfilled the needs and served the purposes there enumerated, then it still fulfils those needs and serves those purposes now. If it is the product of human fear, and the projection of human vanity, then it will still reassure man's nervousness and flatter his egotism. But while it still sustains the rôle which it has sustained through the ages, it will no longer sustain that rôle alone. It will both do more and be more, and the "more" that it does and is will receive adequate interpretation, in so far as it can be interpreted at all, not in terms of the origin and history of religion, but in terms appropriate to its future and its goal. Admittedly, we do not know its future and we can only dimly guess its goal. But of this at least we may be sure, that in the confused complex of tendencies— social and individual, inherited and acquired, instinctive and intellectual—in the vaguely felt aspirations and the scarce acknowledged faith, the sense of spiritual loneliness and the need of spiritual communion, that go to make up what is called religion to-day, there will always be present an element to which the Freudian, or the anthropological, or the social, or any similar account of the appeal and functions of religion will not only not apply, but which it will completely falsify. I say an element, but there is no need to limit my assertion to one. Religion in the past has been a rope of many strands ; it is not likely to grow simple and single in the future. Let us, then, say provisionally that there are two or, perhaps, three aspects or phases of the religious consciousness which none of the subjectivist explanations in terms of the origin and past of religion can explain, and which can be understood only in terms of what religion may become. These aspects we must try to separate from the rest, and, having separated, use as the point of departure for our account of the religion of the future.

To answer the question whether religion is a permanent and necessary growth of the human spirit, and whether as such it will have a future, it is sufficient to point out that there are such aspects. Requiring interpretation in terms of the future rather than the past, it is clear that, as man advances in the path of evolution, they will become more prominent and definite than they are to-day. Religion, therefore, in so far as it contains them, will not die out. To answer the further question what sort of future it may be, it is necessary to disentangle them from the material in which they are embedded, the material which has come to us from religion's origin and past, and consider them in isolation. It is this task which will occupy us in the next two chapters.

Let us in conclusion summarise the results arrived at in this one. When we have to deal with growing and developing things, with living organisms, with the institutions in which they are organised, and the activities in which they find expression, the explanation of their present state in terms of their origin is inadequate. This statement is true both of morals and of religion. To say that the moral consciousness arose because it promoted tribal efficiency, or that the religious consciousness arose because it promoted cosmic comfort, tells us something, but not everything about the moral or the religious consciousness now. To understand them as they are now we must judge them not only by their roots but by their fruits, looking not only to what they have been, but to what they may become. The mind, in short, is Janus-like ; it looks forward as well as backward, bearing upon it at any given moment traces not only of what it has been, but what it may become. And when we come to consider the activities in which it expresses itself, that, for example, of the religious consciousness, we shall find that they contain an element which does not reflect the past, but foreshadows the future.

The conclusion is that there is more in a complex product like the religious consciousness than can be adequately explained by a reference to its origin. This "more" will be a pointer to the future, and we must try, therefore, to disentangle it from the rest, in order to estimate the prospects of religion in the future.

Chapter IX

OUR DUTY TOWARDS OUR NEIGHBOUR

Chapter IX

OUR DUTY TOWARDS OUR NEIGHBOUR

This scheme to thrust forward and establish a human control over the destinies of life and liberate it from its present dangers, uncertainties, and miseries is . . . an altogether practicable one, subject only to one qualification, that sufficient men and women will be willing to serve it.—H. G. WELLS, *The Open Conspiracy*.

If the Catechism is to be believed, the Christian religion includes two duties : there is our duty towards God, and our duty towards our neighbour. In chapter vii. I have glanced at the origins of both—of our duty towards God in man's feeling of loneliness and insignificance in face of the indifference of Nature, and of our duty towards our neighbour in his obligation to observe the implied contract upon which the existence of society depends. In the last chapter I saw reason to doubt whether this account of our religious duties in terms of their origins was complete. Did it, I asked, tell us about them *all* that there was to know, and, in so doing, dispose of the claims of religion to objective truth? Answering that it did not, I must now try to show what more there is in the religious consciousness as it is to-day than its critics are prepared to allow.

Taking the Catechism's hint as to the two elements in religion, I propose to divide my discussion into two parts, dealing respectively with our duty towards God and our duty towards our neighbour. First, however, I must translate the Catechism language into more suitable terms. For me man's duty towards God sums up his relation to the universe as a whole ; his duty to his neighbour, his relations to his fellow-men as a whole. And if we may assume, as most religions do, that there are two worlds, the world in which we pass our daily life, and the world of which we are held to have fleeting glimpses in spiritual and mystical experience, the world of our present and the world of what we may hope will one day be our future

KR

existence, the two main elements in religion define
themselves conveniently enough in terms of our
relation to these two worlds. Our relation to the
first in what I shall call its religious aspect, consists
simply in our duty to make it better ; our relation to
the second in our endeavour, and the endeavour
through us of life as a whole, to know it and, it may
be, to evolve at a level at which we may enter into
communion with it. In the present chapter I shall be
concerned with our relation to the world which we
experience in our day to day life ; in the succeeding
chapter with our relation to the world revealed in
the fleeting intimations of the spirit.

Coming, then, to our duty towards our fellow-men,
the first point that I want to emphasise is that, in
spite of all the evidence to the contrary, we do care
about the happiness of other people, and desire to
increase it, and that, in spite of all the evidence to the
contrary, we do care about the state of the world and
desire to improve it. In the evidence to the contrary I
wish to include all the more obvious truisms, such as,
that we none of us care about these things for all our
time, that few of us care about these things for most
of our time, that most of us care about them for very
little of our time, and a negligible residue perhaps
(limiting cases) for none of our time ; that we often
wish people ill and desire to give them pain ; that on
occasion, e.g., when our livers are out of order or our
lovers unkind, we disinterestedly desire (some of us)
to increase the amount of unhappiness in the world,
and that very few of us ever desire to promote the
happiness of other people when it is likely to interfere with our own. All these things and more may be
admitted. It may be admitted, further, that the disinterested desire for the good of others, and for the
improvement of the world, alive in the young, is
dormant in the middle aged, and, more often than
not, dead in the old. Because people are unable to
express themselves politically and socially, to in-

fluence the lives of their fellows, and to feel that they count in public affairs, they come to seem to others, and in the course of time to themselves, self-centred and cynical, with no interests outside the immediate circles of family and business within which their immediate activities lie. Thus the impulse to do good in the world is thought not to exist, where in most men it has once existed and has become atrophied. The concern for the welfare of others, the desire to make the world a better place, is a flame which burns brightly, even fiercely, in youth, is douched with the cold waters of disillusion and disappointment, flickers uncertainly for a time and goes out. In most old men it is completely extinguished, and to most of us even in middle age there are left of the generous glow of our early youth only the ashes of cynicism and materialism. It should be one of the main tasks of religion to keep that flame alight.

That it is its task is beginning already to be recognised. The Modernists, as I have already pointed out,[1] have given a new interpretation to man's duty to his neighbour, and assigned to it a fuller importance in the religious life. We are to do good in this world, here and now, not because good conduct will win us a good place in the next, but because good conduct is good in itself. And so we find the teaching of the Modernists characterised by a growing interest in life as opposed to doctrine, and by a recognition of the importance of this life for its own sake, without reference to its bearing upon our prospects in another. Religion, as Bishop Barnes repeatedly points out, must evolve. What does that mean, if not that its concern is with the needs of the present and the possibilities of the future, rather than with the dogmas of the past ! Religion, in fact, if it is to survive, must again become a social force, and the religious attitude, instead of being confined, as it has been in the past, to a particular set of activities springing from an isolated

[1] Chapter ii., p. 31.

and unique side of our nature vaguely conceived as spiritual, must permeate every aspect of our personality, and extend into all the avocations of our daily life.

What is required, then, is to bring religion out of the church into the market-place, and a praiseworthy attempt is made to do so, the religious point of view being, for example, defined in relation to the world of business and to industrial disputes.

Concrete expressions of the Modernist movement include community services, the Church support of prohibition in the United States, and the intervention of the Churches in the mining dispute of 1926 in England. The so-called "Bishops' Plan" for the settlement of the dispute, put forward in July, was, though unsuccessful, a good illustration of the Modernist conception of the function of religion in social life.

All this, no doubt, is admirable. It is unfortunate that people do not take it seriously. It may be that it is the destiny of Christianity, it may even be that it is the destiny of the Church of England, to revivify religion by regenerating the world. But it is unlikely. The Churches have to fight not only against the evils of the present, but against the traditions of their own past. Throughout their history they have with singular unanimity ranged themselves on the side of reaction and oppression. Is it credible that they can to-day assume the rôle of the champions of progress and enlightenment ? Can the ecclesiastical leopard change his reactionary spots ? There are men in the Church, admittedly, who would willingly and unsparingly give time and energy to such a cause, who would lay down life itself, if they thought that by doing so they could make the religion of Jesus Christ an effective agent in the building of a better world. There are such men in the Church, there always have been, and they are the salt of the earth. But equally they are, as they always have been, hopelessly unrepresentative of the general body of the paid exponents of the teaching of Christ.

For consider what the social record of the Church has been. It is only a few hundred years ago that priests and theologians were burning by the thousand men and women whom they believed to be in league with the devil, and whom they denounced as the causes of illnesses and thunderstorms, and anything else for which they could not otherwise account. To suggest the slightest alleviation of the prolonged torture of these victims was denounced by educated and cultured clerics of all denominations alike, and practically to a man, as "an offence to God." But I do not want to soil these pages with the horrors of the Church's persecuting past; suffice it, therefore, to say that cruelty both more in quantity and more fiendish in quality has been inflicted by representatives of the religion of Christ (both the Roman Catholic and Protestant varieties of that religion) upon those who have ventured to disagree with them than by any other class of living creature, whether human or animal, upon any other class. This, at least, is the considered judgment of so weighty an authority as Lecky,[1] who concludes several pages of description of the appalling atrocities perpetuated by Christians upon one another in the fifteenth and sixteenth centuries at the instigation of the Church, with the comment that these things were done in the name of Him who commanded his followers to love one another.

Turning our backs upon these horrors, let us consider the Church of England in the last century, when it had largely ceased to be persecuting and had become merely reactionary. Every claim for justice, every appeal to reason, every movement for equality, every proposal to relieve the poverty, to mitigate the

[1] See Lecky's *History of European Morals.*

savagery, or to enlighten the ignorance of the masses
was morally certain to encounter the opposition of
the Church. From many similar instances, I cite a
few at random. The clergy of the Established Church
either actively opposed or were completely indifferent to the abolition of the slave trade. Even the pious
Churchman Wilberforce, writing in 1832, was compelled to admit that "the Church clergy have been
shamefully lukewarm in the cause of slavery abolition." They opposed the movement for the abolition
of the Rotten Boroughs, prophesying that, if the Re-
form Bill of 1832 was carried, it would lead to the
destruction of the Establishment. They opposed in
1806 Whitbread's Bill to establish parish schools in
England out of the rates, the Archbishop complaining
that the proposal would take too much power from
the clergy. State education was indeed persistently
and at all times opposed by the Church, because "it
would enable the labouring classes to read seditious
pamphlets, vicious books, and publications against
Christianity."[1] They opposed the efforts of Joseph
Arch in the seventies to secure better wages for the
half-starved agricultural labourer.

All through the century, whenever and wherever
there is a movement for change and betterment,
the clergy are found opposing it. In this they were
merely carrying on the tradition of their order.
When one looks back over history, one realises that
there is scarcely any discovery which science has
made for human advancement and happiness which
churchmen and theologians have not violently
opposed. Not content with burning each other,
they burnt the men who discovered the earth's
motion, burnt the men who made the first tentative beginnings of physics and chemistry, burnt the
men who laid the foundations of our medical knowledge.

[1] Mr. Giddy, afterwards President of the Royal Society under
the name of Gilbert, in 1807.

When science made it possible to fight smallpox epi-
demics, churchmen opposed the necessary sanitary
measures as an attempt to escape merited punishment, and denounced vaccination as "an offence to
God." When chloroform was invented, they opposed
its use, especially in childbirth—had not God laid a
primæval curse upon woman ?—and denounced it as
"an offence to God." A hundred years ago, when
the discovery of the steam-engine made railways
possible, the clergy preached against them as
"unnatural" and a sin against God. To-day they are
denouncing birth control as "unnatural" and "an
offence to God." In the eighteenth century they opposed the use of lightning conductors as an interfer-
ence with God's intentions, in the sixteenth they
opposed the introduction of forks for use at table, and
denounced them from the pulpit !

Bad as has been the Church's record in the past, it is
not greatly improved in the present. The Church's
opposition to any movement making for social change
is still notorious. Let us take as an example and consider in a little more detail the question of birth control.
The case for birth control is one of the strongest in
modern times. So strong is it, and so familiar are the
arguments in its favour, that it is unnecessary to repeat them here. For the knowledge and facilities
requisite for the control of birth there is an overwhelming demand. Confronted with the fact of this
demand, what is the attitude of the Church ? The
Church has varied between two attitudes. Burying its
head ostrich like in the ecclesiastical sand, it has pre-
tended that it had never heard of the artificial control
of birth, and that there is, therefore, no problem ;
when the fact has been forced upon its attention, it
has disapproved, denounced, and opposed it. The
first is the normal, the second is the official attitude
of the Church, as witness, for example, the following
pronouncement contained in the report of the
Conference of Bishops of the Anglican Communion,

held at Lambeth Palace, 5th July to 7th August,
1920 :

> An emphatic warning is given against the use of unnatural
> means for the avoidance of conception, together with the grave
> dangers—physical, moral, and religious—thereby incurred, and
> against the evils with which the extension of such use threatens
> the race.
> The governing considerations of Christian marriage are its
> primary purpose—the continuation of the race through the gift
> and heritage of children ; and the paramount importance in
> married life of deliberate and thoughtful self-control.

This sounded excellent, but nobody seemed to pay
much attention. On the contrary, as time went on,
morals grew palpably laxer, youth noticeably more
lawless, the list of divorce cases longer, dress more
immodest, while birth control was notoriously spreading among all classes of the community. Something—
it was obvious—must be done about this question of
sex. But, beyond occasionally denouncing the wickedness of youth, or the materalism of the age, the
Church has done nothing. Questions involving sex
occasion, and always have occasioned, the Church
discomfort. Spiritually (it seems difficult to avoid
dropping into the feminine gender at this point) she
blushes when her attention is drawn to them, and, as
soon as may be, averts her eyes, gathers up her skirts,
and passes by on the other side. And so the behaviour
of the Church has, on the whole, been that of the
ostrich. Despite the recommendation of the Lambeth
Conference, her general attitude on the subject of
birth control remains obscure, and most people would
find difficulty in saying what it is. On this, one of the
most important and for many minds perplexing, issues
of the day, she has given no lead at all. So harmful to
the influence of the Church is the effect of this
masterly silence felt to be that in the summer of 1929
the Rev. Edward Lyttelton, late headmaster of Eton,
published a book, *The Christian and Birth Control*,

in which he besought the Church for light and leading. The book, circulated by the S.P.C.K., begins
with an "Open letter to the Bishops." The following
extracts are interesting as showing the distress of an
enlightened Christian, at the hesitancy and vacilla-
tion, to use no stronger words, of the Church.

My Lords,—A certain perplexity in modern life has lately arisen
and assumed a form most acute and most urgent. . . . Far and
wide, almost without exception in every section of our community,
there is bewilderment about the right line of action in the restriction of the size of families, which has been forced upon us by the
social and economic conditions of our time. From that bewilderment and symptomatic of it has arisen the problem loosely entitled
Birth Control.

Elderly people often talk of the lawlessness of the rising generation. But this is a misuse of language. The lawlessness is not on
their part, but on ours. Their conduct exhibits, not violation of the
law, but ignorance of it. They are beset by over-mastering natural
desires inflamed by promptings from every quarter, which, wholly
untrammelled, gather volume day by day. If those to whom they
naturally look as their guides and guardians of their moral life
"keep silence, yea, even from good words" the result is a foregone
conclusion. Who, then, are they that ought to speak ? Who but the
shepherds and bishops of their souls ?

We are all being judged, tested, sifted, when on a great scale a
free but very difficult choice of conduct is presented to the witnesses whom Christ has chosen. Especially is this true when there
is divergence of opinion among our leaders, so that a strong unanimous affirmation seems to be impossible. I cannot believe that the
divergence of opinion among your Lordships is fundamental. As a
test, let this proposition be weighed.

If contraception is not wrong, in many cases it must be right.
Will any pastor of a flock say this from his pulpit ? Will any
Bishop put his name to a document commending the practice,
even to dwellers in the slums ? Why not ? Or will any ordained
minister of God's Word and Sacraments avow in public that he is
himself a contraceptionist ? If not, why not ? It is because the
voice of conscience is still in many quarters believed to be the
Voice of God.

Practically, then, your Lordships, hesitating to affirm, would
actually deny that the matter is serious.

The Rev. Lyttelton goes on to hint that the only

clear and definite lead which it is possible for the Church to give consists in the reaffirmation of the sanctity of marriage, coupled with a general prohibition of contraceptive methods, a prohibition subject to qualification in hard cases. Whatever we may think of the author's own recommendation, we can at least agree with him that a Church which aspired to the moral leadership of the country would at least have the courage to take a definite line. About its attitude, whether right or wrong, there would be no doubt, so that none should have the excuse of ignorance for acting in opposition to its teaching.

The importance of giving a definite lead is realised by the Roman Catholic Church, which, with its usual appreciation of the needs of the situation, thunders in season and out against birth control, and threatens those who practise it with hell fire. "The Church *does* teach that the frustration of the natural consequences of marital life, either by imperfect acts or by the use of artificial means of whatever kind, whether chemical or instrumental, is always a deadly sin, meriting eternal damnation unless sincerely repented of before death." So Dr. Arendzen, stating the Catholic point of view on birth control in a newspaper Symposium. Not so, however, the average Anglican parson. Sharing the Catholic's disapproval, he lacks his outspokenness, so that beyond the feeling, a feeling which with most men has become a kind of instinct (the Church, it is well known, is always opposing and disapproving of something, especially if it is new), that parsons object to birth control, and that the subject had better be avoided in their presence, the average man does not know what the Church's view is, and, not knowing, he does not care. And the feeling of the average man is quite right. Of course the Churches disapprove ; they always do ; but they lack, most of them, the courage to say so. Vaguely but obstinately they oppose divorce and seek to perpetuate the misery of the unhappily married ; and vaguely but obstinately they oppose birth control, and seek to drive working class women to the mad-house or the grave through excess of child bearing. As usual, they are playing Canute to the tide. A day will come when it will seem as strange to our descendants that anyone ever opposed birth control, as it seems strange to us now that serious, intelligent, and well-meaning people ever withheld the mercy of anæsthetics on principle, or for the glory of their God subjected multitudes of their fellow-men and women to the most abominable tortures.

A Church with such a past and such a present does not inspire optimism in regard to its future. Is it really credible that the Anglican Church, as we know it to-day, can take the lead in directing and exploiting the vague enthusiasm for social betterment which animates young men and women, and from which springs that stream of religious feeling which finds expression in our "duty towards our neighbour?" It scarcely seems to. That the idealism, the loyalties, and the self-sacrifice to which this half-unconscious obligation to our fellows gives rise are an integral part of religion I am convinced ; they are probably a growing part, but I doubt if, in spite of the efforts of the Modernists, they will bestow a new lease of life upon the failing faith which is organised in the Church of England.

If, then, as I insist, this social aspect of religion is a real aspect, if, as I believe, it is likely to play an increasingly important rôle in the world of the future, in what form is it likely to express itself ? It is time to return from our digression and to take up the main thread of the argument.

Asserting the existence of disinterested benevolence which dictates the performance of our "duty towards our neighbours," I was careful to protect myself from the cynics by limiting and qualifying my assertion in every possible way. Claiming little more than its bare existence, I admitted that it manifested itself intermittently in the best of us, and that in most of us, particularly after middle age, it has died a natural death. It is difficult to make righteousness readable, difficult to write well of one's fellows, without being written ill of oneself. My theme being disinterested benevolence, I shall do my utmost to keep my righteousness within bounds. Meanwhile, feeling guiltily conscious of the unworldliness of my central assertion, I have squirted round it a little worldly ink for my own satisfaction and the discomfiture of my critics. Having done so, I proceed to reiterate it.

It is, then, my conviction that, other things being equal, we dó, on the whole, desire to do good in the world, and to promote the happiness and well-being of our neighbours. That they rarely are equal is true ; but that is not our fault ; also it is not the point. It is this desire, I say, which lies at the root of our duty towards our neighbour, and expresses itself in what, for the sake of a better word, I shall call the political impulse. It is a desire which all of us experience in greater or less degree because we are men ; if a man did not possess it, he would be, in respect of his deficiency, not wholly and completely a man. Nor should its existence occasion surprise. Man, after all, is a political and social being who has lived for the past five hundred generations in society. And, since the prosperity and misfortunes of society produce an undeniable effect for good or ill upon the individual, it is only natural, to put the matter on its lowest ground, that the individual should care about the well-being of those who with himself constitute what is called society.

But this is to interpret in terms of origins, and in this chapter we are concerned with those expressions of the human spirit which cannot be so interpreted. Refusing, then, to put the matter at its lowest, we shall recognise simply that we all of us on occasion have the *salus populi* deeply at heart, and do, in spite of all appearances to the contrary, concern ourselves about the happiness and welfare of others, especially of those others who happen to be poor and oppressed.

Concerned with the welfare of our neighbours, we desire to influence their lives and to influence them in the direction which seems to us to be good. That we are often mistaken as to what is for their good, and that, whether we are mistaken or not, they rarely agree with us, is true but irrelevant. But it is not enough to be interested in the "well-being of the people" if you are powerless to improve their lives, or even to set before them your own conception of how life ought to be lived. Hence arises the almost universal desire for some sort of influence or control, however limited, in the affairs of society. Men wish to feel somehow that they count, that their thoughts and actions matter, and that it is not beyond the bounds of possibility that some one of their thoughts or actions might really influence society, and be of service to their fellow-men.

For this desire the structure of modern society makes little provision ; its existence is unwillingly recognised—witness the discouragement by old and respectable persons of Socialism in the young—and, when recognised, it is denied expression. Nor can it easily secure it. One of the chief drawbacks of the modern State is its size. So vast are the forces at work in society, so complex and elaborate the structure of Government, and so intricate and difficult to disentangle the different strands that condition events, that, so far from controlling them, men are unable even to understand them. In face of the complex organisation of society, the individual feels impotent. Events which occur seem to be not so much the result of human will and effort, as of the interplay of blind and uncontrollable forces whose genesis escapes detection, and whose object, if any, is shrouded in mystery. Men are driven more and more to that interpretation of phenomena with which Mr. Hardy's novels have made us familiar, to the notion of a blind, unthinking Thing, will-less and purposeless, which determines the march of events without plan or purpose, and, as it fares remorselessly on its appointed way, furthers human efforts without purpose and thwarts them without malignity ; a Thing before whose power man's endeavour is powerless, or, if it succeeds, successful by chance and not from intrinsic merit.

And this conception is thrust upon men not through an intellectual adhesion to the doctrines of determinism, nor from any spiritual flirting with fatalism, but simply from the spectacle of a social mechanism so vast that the individual man seems powerless to modify its workings or to mould its ends. It is this notion of a canvas too big for human designs that seems to have inspired Mr. Keynes's famous comment on the working of the forces that made the Versailles Treaty : "One felt most strongly the impression described by Tolstoy in *War and Peace*, or by Hardy in *The Dynasts*, of events marching on to their fated conclusion uninfluenced and unaffected by the cerebrations of statesmen in council." It is the size of the machine which thwarts the individual's impulse to pull his weight in society, and not some peculiar characteristic of social affairs which renders them necessarily unamenable to human control.

As a result of this feeling of impotence, the impulse to politics either perishes from inanition, or becomes diverted into side-channels whose outlets would be humorous if they were not pathetic. Those whose impulses seek an emotional rather than an intellectual outlet, whose hearts are, in common parlance, better than their heads, seek in social work and meddling with the morals of the poor that satisfaction which they fail to find in bona fide political activity. The respect which their superior culture, manners, and wealth obtain for them amongst the lower classes creates the fiction that here at last is to be found a sphere of influence in which their talent may find an outlet in activities which are as pleasant as they are salutary. Thus the political impulse finds its vent in investigating the habits of the poor, cataloguing their deficiencies, stigmatising their wastefulness, and distributing coal and blankets to mitigate the more acute forms of distress among the deserving.

Those whose characteristics are pre-eminently intellectual, whose heads are better than their hearts, finding that the magnitude and impersonality of the forces that govern society deny their talents their natural scope in the control and improvement of the lives of others, sink into the soured cynicism, satirical flippancy, and political apathy which are so characteristic of the intelligentsias of the modern world. They cry sour grapes at politics, stigmatise it as a dirty game in which the stakes are personal ambition instead of the welfare of the community, and, like the Russian intellectuals in the last years of the Tsardom, take refuge in dilettantism, psycho-analysis, and the pursuit of art for art's sake. The characters in Tchekov's plays provide a good illustration of the lassitude of intellectuals whose energies are denied legitimate expression in public affairs. Failing to obtain recognition in a world in which the main passport to eminence is a vulgar self-advertisement and a cultivation of the arts of popular appeal and display, they are forced to save their self-respect by making a virtue of their impotence. Ostentatiously they abandon interest in the affairs of society, and seek consolation in love, in art, and personal intrigue.

About art, they urge, there is something quintessential and sublime, which invests it with a reality which is greater than the illusory interests of the world of common men. "Personal relations," they cry with Mr. E. M. Forster in *Howard's End*, "are the real life for ever and ever," and devote themselves to the cultivation and analysis of their friends. As for love, it is, as Aldous Huxley has pointed out, for persons of intelligence the best of indoor sports.

The intellectuals having withdrawn, the direction of society passes to other and less worthy hands. The popular platform, grown too big for the still small voice of reason, is captured by Cleon the leather-lunged, who in a class conscious democracy achieves power by exploiting the simple emotions of greed, hatred, and intolerance.

These are the diseases of democracy ; they grow more apparent as the State grows larger and civilisation more complex, and young men and women, driven by the urge of a political impulse seeking expression, are beginning to take arms against them. One of the most marked features of social life since the war has been the coming together of young men and women inspired by the spirit of service, and seeking in comradeship and community of purpose some substitute for the purely individualistic and self-seeking standards which dominate the lives of their elders. In its milder forms the movement issues in a new return to nature. Originating in Germany, where youth's dissatisfaction with the ways of its elders has been sharpened by the bitterness of defeat, the return to nature has become one of the most distinctive features of the national life. Organised in the Wandervogel, young Germans have turned their backs upon the cities, and, scorning money-making and abjuring ambition, sought and found a simpler and more comradely life on the roads and in the woods. Even in England the movement grows apace. The British Federation of Youth, a body with an aggregate membership of over 50,000, reports that tramps, rambles, week-end camps, visits to permanent country hostels and guest-houses, and so forth, are becoming an increasingly important part of its work. Interwoven with this movement are the week-end schools and the extended summer schools run by youth organisations. Those who are familiar with this back-to-the-country movement agree that it is producing a new attitude of mind amongst those who take part in

it. On long tramps across Europe, or it may be on a
series of week-end walks, the members of a group of
young people will come to know each other with an
intimacy denied to urban acquaintances, and make
the first tentative beginnings of community life. If
this is to be done successfully, tact, mutual understanding, mutual respect, self-control, and self-discipline must be shown by each member of the group.
Thus arises a new conception of the possibilities of
social life. It is this attempt to communalise life which
runs like a continuous thread through the various
activities of modern youth. Whether in pleasure or in
work, in play or in study, young people to-day are
attempting to co-operate. Having emancipated themselves from the narrow home circle, they find their
liberty unsatisfying unless they can learn to enjoy it
in common. The task is a difficult one ; there are
many failures. But clearly it is worth while. In the
past the child and the youth were too often virtually
prisoners in a narrow family circle. They left that
circle only when they married and themselves formed
a new home, soon to be peopled with its new generation of prisoners. First as prisoners, then as jailers,
they spent all their lives in captivity. In such conditions even the first steps towards community life were
impossible. To-day there is the hope born of a new
opportunity ; to-day we are seeing the first fumbling
endeavours at community living.

This coming together of youth in comradeship in
work and in play is, if I am right, a hesitating expression of that political impulse which I have identified with one aspect of the religious spirit. But the
renaissance of modern youth is not limited to country
rambles and week-end talks. It has other and more
definitely political aspects. The insurgence of youth
in politics is irreparably bound up with the decline
of democracy, and it will be necessary to preface
what I have to say with a few observations on that
decline.

LR

I have spoken above of the political apathy of the modern citizen in face of the size and complexity of the modern State. He is apathetic because he realises that he does not count, because he feels that his will cannot be made to matter. And yet—and this is the paradox of modern society—Government proceeds upon the assumption that he does count and that his will does matter. Modern democracy, in fact, is a device for giving to the people the appearance, but not the reality of power. The people, like the king, govern in theory, but not in practice. But because in theory they are the source of power, because those who govern are in theory their representatives, the people, in fact, determine the kind of questions which Governments discuss, or, rather, those which they do not discuss. The electorate takes a small and diminishing interest in politics. Yet it determines the questions in which politicians must interest themselves.

This sounds cryptic, and I must elaborate further. The electorate, I affirm, is politically apathetic—the fact is obvious. Sixty years ago, when the exercise of the vote was the prerogative of the privileged classes, it paid the newspapers to print verbatim reports of parliamentary proceedings. The electorate, though small, was interested. To-day it is often impossible to tell from a perusal of the morning paper whether Parliament is sitting. Those who elect no longer desire to know the sayings and doings of those whom they elect. Nevertheless, from time to time those who are elected have to catch and hold the interest of the electorate. Why ? In order that they may be elected again. To secure re-election they must speak of the things that appeal to the electors, and upon the success of their appeal on these occasions their careers depend. They return to power with a mandate to proceed with the measures which have formed the issues at the election, to do, that is to say, the things that have seemed attractive to the electorate. Thus the issues that have caught the interest of the electors come to be the issues which chiefly occupy the attention of democratically elected Governments.

What are the issues that catch the interest of an apathetic electorate ? They find vent in cries such as "Hang the Kaiser," scares like the Zinovieff letter, or vindictive meannesses like, "Make Germany pay." Yet these are not matters with which the Government of a great country can afford to be concerned. And the defect of modern democracy is just this, that the questions with which it ought to be concerned are too difficult and too technical to arouse the enthusiasm, or even to secure the attention, of the modern voter. Or they win his interest only to offend his prejudices. For example, the first duty of a modern Government is to prevent war. Another war, it is obvious, will destroy our civilisation. It is equally obvious that it is only by the subordination of individual States to the arbitrament of some central international authority that war can be prevented. Yet this essential measure is one which no popularly elected statesman dare advocate ; it would outrage national pride and offend the patriotism of the electors.

Again, it is essential to the well-being of modern civilisation that the optimum population, both for the world and for individual States, should be determined and steps taken to control the birth rate in accordance with the estimate reached. But no responsible statesman dare even discuss, far less advocate such a measure ; it would shock the moral sentiments of the electors.

Again, the world control and rationing of raw materials by a central economic board is an indispensable condition of the peaceful and harmonious development of civilisation. It is the only alternative to Imperialism, and the wars to which Imperialism inevitably leads. Yet the subject is dull and technical, the necessary arrangements complex, and the arguments for the proposal not such as to lend themselves to popular exposition upon the election platform ;

hence it is not mentioned. Instances could be multiplied indefinitely. The matters which are really essential to the security of our precariously poised civilisation are not those with which democratic Governments concern themselves, because they are not those which arouse the enthusiasm of popular electorates. They are too complex and difficult to understand, or too shocking and unpatriotic to discuss. Thus, modern democracy, though lacking the substance of positive power, does, in fact, exercise power negatively by determining the kind of matters with which Governments concern themselves, and, what is more important, those with which they do not.

Now, as I pointed out above, the government of a modern State is an increasingly complex and intricate business. It is a matter for experts. So delicate are the adjustments upon which modern society rests, so far-reaching the ramifications of apparently insignificant governmental actions, that it becomes increasingly difficult to know what should be done, if only because of the difficulty of determining what is likely to be the effect of what is done. The world—it is a commonplace—has become one economic unit. The discovery of oil springs in the Caucasus may throw English miners out of work, and a strike in a Japanese silk factory may render a spinster living in a Bournemouth boarding-house incapable of paying her bill. In a word, what is done anywhere tends to have reverberations everywhere. Thus, while the work of government grows more intricate as society grows more complex and States increasingly interdependent, the democracy whose business it is to cope with it becomes increasingly incapable of understanding the problems that arise. In a modern community it is impossible to determine what the results of a given policy may be. Hence a tentative and experimental attitude to politics is desirable. Yet the modern politician, if he is to win the suffrages of the electors, must profess a dogmatic certainty as to the absolute rightness of certain policies, which have not been tried, while his opponent must be equally certain of their wrongness. The politician ought to be able to say, "I am rather inclined to think that the tax on certain raw materials should be lowered. I am not sure of this, but I am inclined to try it. I shall make the experiment for eighteen months, and, if I turn out to be wrong, shall revise or review the policy." But what he has to say is, "No duties, no tariffs!" "Free trade in everything!" and act as if he believed it. Democracy, in short, assumes that the average citizen is capable of grasping more complex issues than is, in fact, the case, that he is born free and equal, that he has in theory all the wisdom that government requires, and that, utilising this wisdom, he wishes to exercise through his chosen representatives the various powers of Government.

There is, as we have seen, no warrant for these assumptions. On the contrary, the average elector, apathetic and helpless in the vast mechanism of the modern State, is bored with political questions, so bored that his interest can only be momentarily roused by election stunts. Hence politics become for him a matter of golden promises and capricious revenges, of taxing the brewers or the motorists or the landlords, of free breakfast-tables, and making Germany pay. These are not the issues which affect the life of the community, and the conclusion is, therefore, forced upon us that democracy is and will increasingly become incapable of carrying on the functions of government. And, dimly sensing its incapacity, it becomes increasingly incapable. Hence democracy moves in a vicious circle. The electorate is too uninstructed politically to cope with the problems that beset the modern State. The State accordingly functions without its intervention ; and, seeing the State proceeding on its way without reference to his will or his wishes, the ordinary man becomes discouraged, and, losing interest in politics, becomes more politically uninstructed than before. Thus, while the task

of statesmanship becomes increasingly difficult, those
in whom the power theoretically resides become increasingly unfitted for the task. To guide the ship of
State aright through the shoals that beset it there is
required a clear conception of the perils ahead, and a
conscious and continuously directive purpose to
avoid them. Is it conceivable that such direction can
result from the haphazard decision of the ballot-box,
given once every five years upon insignificant issues
dressed up as "questions of the day" to catch the
votes of a fundamentally bored electorate? One
might as well select engineers to build a bridge by
taking a flapper's plebiscite on the most handsome
film faces among Hollywood males.

At this point youth intervenes, and in the course of
its intervention reveals itself as animated by the
closest approximation to the religious spirit that this
generation has known.

One of the most marked features of social life since
the war is the new determination to take a hand in
public affairs which has evinced itself in young men
and women, a determination to take a hand which
speedily tends to become a determination to take
control. This determination is the strength, if it is
not the source of Fascism and of Bolshevism, and it
is the negation of democracy as the Liberalism of the
nineteenth century understood democracy. Im-
pressed on the one hand by the incompetence of
democracy to handle the affairs of a modern community, and discouraged, on the other, by the apathy
and helplessness to which the size and complexity of
the State condemns the citizen who is content to play
the political game according to democratic rules,
groups of young men have taken the political bit between their teeth and sought to impose their will upon
the community whether it liked it or not. On the
whole, it has disliked it less than might have been
supposed. It has protested, but it has protested less
violently than the admirers of democracy had led us

to expect. Throughout Europe to-day there is a growing distrust of constitutional government and a willingness to try new forms, which suggest that the present generation is more prepared to be experimented with than its fathers. The willingness is no doubt in part the result of the apathy to which I have already referred, the average citizen having come to rate politics as of too little importance to him personally to warrant his caring much under what form of Government he lives. Whether he cares or not has been a matter of comparative indifference to the ardent spirits who are resolved to govern him for his good. For they have not professed to express the voice of the people ; they have not even sought to obtain a majority. The people, they have urged, are too ignorant to know, or too soft to do what is necessary, even did they know. Disavowing, therefore, the democratic belief in persuasion as a bourgeois superstition, and prepared to compel where they are unable to convert, they have felt so certain of the rectitude of their aims and the justice of their cause, so convinced that they alone possessed the cure for which the ills of post-war society were clamouring, that they have not hesitated to insist that society should take their medicine whether it would or no.

Successfully to insist, they have needed force, and, needing it, they have not scrupled to use it. Now, the successful use of force involves discipline, and one of the most interesting characteristics of the post-war type of young men of whom I am speaking has been their willingness, in pursuit of their ideals, to subject themselves to discipline. Rejecting the ordinary sensual existence with which most members of a prosperous Western community identify the good life, disdaining to amass large quantities of money, and foregoing ambition and a worldly career, they have been willing in peace-time to undergo the hardships of the soldier in war. Like him, they have put themselves, their lives, and their fortunes unreservedly at the disposal of some external authority ; like him, they have obeyed orders and submitted to training ; and, like him, they have been prepared to face danger and death in the service of their cause. Unlike him, they are austere, living simply, drinking little or not at all, reasonably monogamous and eschewing intimacies with women outside the marriage tie. In their aims and ambitions, in their habits in little things and their resolves in big ones, in their way of life and willingness for death, in their work and their play, they are as different as possible from the ordinary soft citizen of the ordinary industrial democratic community. They are men devoted, and the cause to which they have devoted themselves is the regeneration of society. Thus they acknowledge their duty towards their neighbour.

That these, or something like them, are the ideals with which militant young men have been imbued, and that, pursuing them, they have profoundly influenced the social structure, the history of several European countries since the war bears ample witness.

Naturally they have had most success in those countries which, having suffered most from the war, found themselves most incompetent to deal with the legacy of problems it left behind it. Only in Italy and Russia (and possibly to some extent in Spain) have they actually captured the Governments ; but similar movements are afoot in all countries, and merely bide their time until the folly of another war or some overwhelming economic catastrophe has sapped the prosperity and shattered the self-complacency of the citizens.

Now, these movements are essentially disinterested. They may be wrong-headed, they may be tyrannical and reactionary, unsuited to the needs of the time and inimical to progress, but they are inspired in the main by the wish to promote what their members conceive to be the good of society and not the personal ambitions of those who compose them.

In their conception of that good, they are, I believe, profoundly mistaken. So far as political ends are concerned I am an old fashioned Liberal in the wide, a Socialist in the strict sense, regarding liberty and equality, freedom for the expression of every variety of thought and every shade of opinion, and a respect for the rights and the privacy of the individual as paramount social goods. On the economic side I desire to see an equal distribution of material wealth, and would rank myself a supporter of Shaw's programme of equal incomes for all, irrespective of services rendered to the community. Of these social ends which I hold to be valuable, one only, that of equal distribution of material goods, seems to be held in honour in Bolshevik Russia, and even this seems to be less, rather than more, likely to be realised as Bolshevism settles down. For the rest, I see no attempt to achieve any of the other ends of value I have mentioned by those whose methods I have described. On the contrary, they countenance violence and intolerance, restrict freedom of thought and speech, and exalt the State above the individual, with the result that I know not whether the more to admire the loyalty, the discipline, and the self-sacrifice of the young men by whose endeavours the post-war Governments of Italy and Russia have come to power, or to deplore the ends which these qualities have been employed to serve.

But this is no place for a discussion, still less for a criticism, of the aims and methods of Bolshevism and Fascism, and I do not propose to embark upon it. Indeed, it is irrelevant to my subject, which is the manifestation of what I have called the political impulse (and hence of religion in so far as the political impulse is an expression of religion) in modern society, and its probable development in the future.

And here let me emphasise the point that these movements of militant and disciplined youth, these expressions of the community spirit in the endeavour to promote what is thought to be the good of the community, seem to me essentially religious. They represent an attempt to do one's duty towards one's neighbour because it is one's duty. And, estimating the future of religion, or, rather, of this aspect of religion, I should say that it rests with these and similar movements of young men and women of all countries, inspired by these and similar emotions; but not, I hope, directed to similar ends.

It is not, I repeat, the ends of Bolshevism and Fascism that seem to me to be good; it is the spirit which animates those who pursue them, or who pursued them in their days of unpopularity and danger, that I find admirable. What are the enduring social goods? Peace and toleration, justice and equity, the education and enlightenment of all citizens. Cannot we harness some of the energy and enthusiasm that has animated Communism and Fascism, cannot we command some small part of the loyalty and self-sacrifice that have been lavished so ungrudgingly in the cause of human suffering in pursuit of these ends? Can we not utilise the religious spirit to promote what is good? It seems not.

It is one of the tragedies of humanity that man's noblest qualities have usually been called forth in defence of ends that are harmful. Just as the intensity with which men have embraced their beliefs has usually been in inverse proportion to their truth, so the self-sacrificing idealism which they have displayed in pursuit of their ends has been usually in inverse proportion to the value of the ends pursued. Men have collectively suffered torments in order to go to heaven or to convert the Jews; but very little for the sake of spreading knowledge, and scarcely at all to promote happiness or to produce beauty.

This is unfortunate, and it is worth while considering why our collective endeavours should be so ill-advised. Most of men's social activities have been undertaken under compulsion by powerful persons.

As civilisation develops persuasion has succeeded to compulsion, and the arts of propaganda to those of force. Except when we are hard pressed, as in the late war, we now mould men's minds instead of coercing their bodies. But the change of method has not diminished the power of the few to lead the many. Very much the contrary ! In a modern community the influence of leaders increases as the avenues of propaganda multiply, while the effect of education in giving people the power to read but not to criticise what they read is to make them the dupes of unscrupulous advertisement.

It is still true, therefore, as it has always been, that the actions of great bodies of men are determined by the wishes of the ruling few. Now, the ends which most rulers have wished to pursue have been in the main harmful. Of the collective passions of dominant individuals or groups, the strongest have historically been the desire for wealth and power. These they have sought to acquire and increase at the expense of the wealth and power of rival individuals and groups. Thus ambition coupled with fear and hatred have been the dominant motives of most governing class activities. For this reason the ends which people's energies have been employed to secure, being the ends of powerful individuals or groups, have been in the main evil. But the motives from which they have been led to put forth their energies have been good, and it has been by appeals to the best rather than to the worst that is in them that rulers have been able to enlist their effective support. Most men will put forth greater efforts in the cause of what they believe to be right than they will do to advance their own personal interests. They will also suffer more. Hence, to get the most out of their followers, leaders have always found it prudent to make out a good moral case for the course of action proposed.

In the Middle Ages those respectable burghers who tortured witches did so, not because they were cruel, but because they desired to save witches from the clutches of the devil. The Inquisition persecuted and burnt heretics, not because its priests took a delight in distorted limbs and roasted living flesh, but because they were persuaded that it was only by this means that the heretics would escape an eternity of burning in hell. And in modern times it is by appeals, not to their cupidity or to their cruelty, but to their idealism that decent people are induced to further the schemes of scoundrels, in the belief that they are fighting for justice and liberty.

Enlightened persons frequently contrast the hundreds of millions that a modern nation spends on armaments with the paltry thousands that it is willing to give to education, to housing, or to hygiene. But the contrast is not confined to expenditure. Men will not only give more money, they will give more time, more energy, more ardour and enthusiasm to killing and coercing their fellows than to educating them, to housing them, to keeping them healthy, or to tending them when they are sick. To the work of destruction they will bring a nobility, a forgetfulness of self, a truly religious spirit which the work of construction is powerless to evoke. Thus, were it not for the good in men, most of the evil in the world would have remained undone.

Let us consider in this connection in a little more detail the case of war. Of all the evil ends to promote which men have given themselves, of all the false ideals that have called forth their loyalty and self-sacrifice, of all the bad things for the sake of which they have done bad things from the best motives, war is assuredly the worst. To kill men that you have never seen and with whom you have no quarrel (the enemy !) because other men whom you have never seen and do not necessarily respect (the Government) tell you that you ought to want to do so, of all the strange activities of civilised manhood this assuredly is the strangest ! One knows not whether to be the more appalled at its wickedness or amazed at its folly. Yet war, as its apologists are never tired of telling us, has called forth more courage and endurance, has enlisted in its service more nobility and unselfishness, than any other human institution. The suffering and sacrifice and uncomplaining heroism which war alone has demanded, had they only been given to causes which manhood deems ignoble, could in the million years of man's existence have eliminated the need for suffering anywhere within his sphere of activity. War alone can make men trained in the school of self-assertiveness forget the good of the individual in the good of all. War is the one thing that can unite men ; it is also the one thing they all know to be wrong.

In the early days of the Great War there blew through men the wind of a spirit which was the nearest thing to religion that this age has seen. They enjoyed that sense of fellowship and of community of working for a common cause that in peace-time they had not known, and, enjoying it, were ready for any sacrifice. Each man thought of himself as a molecule in the body of a community that was engaged in discharging an obligation of honour. France was to be saved, Belgium righted, freedom re-won, a soured, crooked old world rid of bullies and reclaimed for straightness and decency and good-nature. And, fighting for these things, they felt themselves members of a team ; they had got themselves happily placed on a rope at which everyone else was tugging his best as well as they. And from men, uplifted by this common cause, enjoying this sense of fellowship, all the worries and burdens of their isolation seemed magically to have fallen away. There were no longer any difficult choices to be made, no pass-books to con, nobody's fate to settle, not even one's own. For all was fixed and provided for down to the times of one's rising and going to bed, the number of buttons on one's coat, and the way of lacing one's boots.

This vow of willing enslavement which every man had voluntarily made, this allegiance to a cause transcending his own interests, this recognition of a will outside his own, had transformed him from a nervous little clod of vanities and ailments, torn by desires, weighed down by responsibilities and harassed by conflicting claims, and given him the blitheness of heart that comes of the tranquil acquiescence in the merging of the self in something greater than the self, the peace that passeth understanding that belongs as surely to the youngest volunteer as to the mystic and the saint. Lapped in the repose of utter obedience, men sang in the morning, ate like hunters, and rediscovered the instinctive joy in life of which modern civilisation had robbed them. And they forgot that they were individuals separated by class distinctions ; they remembered only that they were working together on a common job. And, so remembering, they attained happiness. Their spirits were cleansed, their bodies rejuvenated ; they were twice the men they were before.

It has been my lot in recent years to be brought into contact as a teacher with many young men and women in the early twenties. They have been for the most part engaged in clerical work of minor importance in Government or big business offices ; some have been school teachers, others bank-clerks, others salesmen, and there has been a sprinkling of young manual workers. Their work absorbs but a small part of their energies and satisfies none of their aspirations. They regard it for the most part as task work, as seven or eight hours of not too arduous drudgery to be performed every day before they can begin to live. Having performed it, they leave their offices, fresh and eager, with energies untapped and appetites unsated for what life may have to offer them.

Of religion in the ordinary sense of the word they have none. In an average company of them, not one, as I had occasion to mention earlier in this work, will be found to believe in God, and scarcely any will feel a need to believe.

But they have an appetite for intellectual adventure ; they are not afraid of arduous intellectual effort ; they are alight with generous enthusiasms, and they have a great fund of goodwill. Fundamentally they wish their neighbours well, and, keenly alive to the evils of the society in which their lot is cast, would not spare themselves in the effort to make it better. In them is the same capacity for self-sacrifice, for self-forgetfulness in some cause which is recognised to be worth while, for social service and for disinterested endeavour, which has been the driving-force behind Bolshevism and Fascism, and helped these movements to win through from unpopularity to power.

But they do not subscribe to the political ideals either of Russian Communism or of Italian Fascism, and they are not organised. Meanwhile, they move in groups and circles, are full of windy enthusiasms, as soon forgotten as conceived, and beat about the cage of life like any other wild thing newly captured. To put it crudely, they don't know what to do with themselves, and give to wireless, to sport, and to sexual experimentation the energy that should be utilised in the service of their fellows.

In a dozen years' time they will be middle-aged men and women with families and homes ; their horizon will be bounded by trivial cares, their aspirations limited to the furthering of petty ambitions and the achievement of an animal content, and in the end, after a brief period of disillusion and despair relieved perhaps by a series of sporadic love affairs, they will settle down into a state of resignation, and, after a decade of resentful recognition of the fact that they cannot get what they like, will grow ultimately to like what they get, having forgotten that they were ever capable of liking anything better. In a word, they will have ceased to be citizens and become units, whom nothing will any longer have the power of lifting up out of the selfish little pit of vanity and desire which is the self into something which is greater than the self.

What I have described is commonplace enough ; it is nothing more than the process of youth's subsidence into middle age. I have seen it repeated again and again, and, until we discover some means of tapping and utilising for the good of society the political impulse which wells up in our finer young men, it will be repeated indefinitely.

In concluding this chapter, therefore, I want to ask if it is not, after all, possible to conserve and utilise this political impulse, which I have sought to identify with one aspect of religion, to conserve and utilise it not only for the good of society, but in the interests of the individual himself ? If I am right, the aspect of religion which expresses itself in our duty towards our neighbour has a special importance to-day, and for three reasons. First, the modern generation is, as I have repeatedly pointed out, to all intents and purposes without religious beliefs, and religion in the ordinarily understood sense of the word plays no part in its life. Religion has flourished in some form or another among all peoples in all previous ages of the world's history. This could not have been the case unless it answered to a deep-seated longing, and provided expression for a universal need of human nature. We cannot suppose that the present generation is an evolutionary "sport," different from all preceding generations, in the sense that a desire and a need previously so widespread as to be practically universal have in it suddenly disappeared. If it is not, it follows that the desire and the need must not only exist, but remain to a large extent unsatisfied. In the souls of young people to-day the decline of orthodox religion has left a vacuum, and it ought to be filled.

Secondly, religion, as we have known it in this country, has in the past provided a special channel for the expression of what I have called the political impulse, in the corporate life which has gathered round the church, and still more the chapel, as its centre. In this life humble people have been able to develop their social natures in relation to their fellows, and to realise something at least of what they have it in them to be, sensing and in part fulfilling their duty, not to their neighbour in the widest sense, but to their neighbour in the community that centred round their place of worship. In it they found opportunity for the development of talents and the gratification of instincts denied expression elsewhere. It is not too much to say that the political capacity which in the palmy-days of nineteenth century democracy was at once the pride and the distinction of the self-conscious citizen, was usually developed in some little Bethel. Effort and endeavour that subsequently found their way into trade union and co-operative adventures were first put forth in chapel communities, where men first learnt to trust, to help, and to work with their fellows.[1] To-day these little worlds have practically disappeared, and, where they persist, they have lost vitality. They have subsided into tea-parties and mothers' meetings ; they no longer afford an avenue of expression for the political impulse, and too often modern society offers nothing in their stead.

Yet some equivalent avenue of self-expression is more necessary than it has ever been before, because —and this is my third reason—of the deadening effect of the modern State upon the individual. He is a cog in a vast machine which grinds on to its appointed end irrespective of his wishes, and often, it seems, indifferent to his weal or woe. He wants to feel that he counts ; yet there is nothing that he can do, no point at which he can take hold. Hence arises a sense of bafflement and helplessness, and the political impulse is thwarted and driven underground.

[1] See Trevelyan's *British History in the Nineteenth Century,* p. 160.

MR

The individual as a result tends to be an isolated unit ; he has no sense of corporate responsibility, and he misses the joy of working with others for a common cause. It is easy to see in retrospect why so many men experienced a great and uplifting joy of fellowship, a sense of exaltation new to them when training with the army in the early days of the war. They were experiencing for the first time the pleasure of shared activities in what was thought to be a worthy cause. Working both with and for their fellows, they liberated the political impulse within them.

Many times I have been asked in these latter years by young men and women, anxious to take a hand in the job of making the world afresh, what they can do. Faced by this question, I may have made some vague reference to Wells's *Open Conspiracy*, I may have urged them to attend W.E.A. Classes or to join I.L.P. branches. But these things—I have known it as I advised them—are mere makeshifts, and in the last resort I have been compelled to admit that I do not know. For—and this is the tragedy of the young man of to-day—there is nothing that he can do.

This, then, is the task of religion in the modern world, to capture the imaginations of young men and women, as the Bolsheviks have captured them in Russia and the Fascists in Italy ; to harness their energies and to utilise their enthusiasms, to find expression, in a word, for the political impulse as Communism and Fascism have succeeded in expressing it, but to do these things not for ends that are harmful, but in the service of what is socially and politically good. To translate into old-fashioned terminology, religion must make of our duty towards our neighbour an instrument to establish the Kingdom of Heaven upon earth.

Chapter X

OUR DUTY TOWARDS GOD

Chapter X

OUR DUTY TOWARDS GOD

Our assurance of God is a consciousness of a relation rather than a flawless proof of existence.[1]

I do not believe that our experience is the highest form of experience extant in the universe. I believe rather that we stand in just the same relation to the whole universe as our canine and feline pets do to the whole of human life. They inhabit our drawing-rooms and libraries ; they take part in scenes of whose significance they have no inkling. They are small tangents to curves of history the beginnings and ends of which pass wholly beyond their ken. So are we tangents to the wider things of life.—W. JAMES.

I come now to a chapter which I find it very difficult to write. In it I want to say in what for me the essence of religion consists ; and for me the essence of religion is mysticism. Now mysticism, from the very fact that it is mysticism, cannot give an account of itself. If it could, it would cease to be mysticism. This is unfortunate in a world which becomes increasingly explanatory ; yet on reflection it is seen to be inevitable. Language was invented to serve the purposes of human beings living in a material world of people and things ; its intention is strictly practical. How, then, can it be appropriately employed to describe the nature and uses of a world containing neither ? And yet, if mysticism means anything at all, if it is not the illegitimate projection into a passive universe of the morbid imaginings of the sexually starved, the psychologically perverted, or the merely insane, it must seek to give some account of the venturings of the human spirit into another world, and of such communion with it as in his present state of evolution man has been able to achieve.

Faced with the necessity of giving an account of other-worldly experiences in words invented to serve

[1] Professor Eddington, lecturing to the Society of Friends, May 1929.

the purposes of daily life, the mystic, perforce, must resort to the language of metaphor, in the hope that some of his similes will strike a responsive chord in others. This, on the whole, they have noticeably failed to do. Nor should this failure cause surprise. Mysticism, if I am right, is a private and personal experience, as private and as personal as the toothache. As such it is incommunicable except to those who have shared, in however slight a degree, experiences of the same sort as those which it seeks to record. You cannot, it is obvious, convey what the sensation of having the toothache is like to one who has never had it.

For this reason the generality of mystics have consistently talked what is to most of us manifest nonsense. "It neither moves nor rests," they say, and speak of "a dazzling darkness" or "a delicious desert." Such contradictory statements must, it is thought, be the vapourings of men bemused. And, stigmatising them as such, we have been prepared contemptuously to dismiss mysticism as moonshine, when we ought to have contented ourselves with regretfully remarking the fact that there was no chord in our experience which could be made to vibrate responsively to the mystic's utterance. Yet to dismiss mysticism as nonsense because we cannot comprehend the utterances of individual mystics, is like supposing that all foreigners are mad because we cannot understand what they say. It is mere intellectual parochialism.

For the mystic, as for the artist, his revelation is a psychological fact ; like colour, or sound, heat, or shape, it is undeniably a part of his experience ; it is there ; it is real. Admittedly his experience is different from that of most of us ; but so is an artist's—obviously, since he records it—or a dog's or a barnacle's. And what claim, after all, has the world revealed to the eyes of twentieth-century common sense to be the sole type of reality ? It is negligible ! Science and

philosophy combine to discredit the reality of objects
of everyday experience, dissolving chairs and tables
into a whirl of dancing electrons, mathematical events
in a spatio-temporal continuum, colonies of souls or
ideas in the mind of the observer. The world of common sense is a conventional construction, a legacy
from man's philosophical past; common sense itself a
mass of dead metaphysics. Most of us, admittedly, find
it convenient to construct the common-sense world
alike because we have similar interests and similar
sense organs. But slightly change the condition of our
sense organs, and how differently it appears. We have
only, for example, to raise the temperatures of our
bodies five degrees, for sight and sounds, tastes and
smells, to acquire a new significance. Above all, the
world we touch, or rather that touches us, is radically
changed ; it is richer, more insistent, and more varied.
Yet because a man's temperature is temporarily above
normal, nobody would say that his sensations are not
really felt, or that the world they reveal to him has
not as much right to be called real as that which is experienced by bodies with temperatures at 98·4 Fahr-
enheit. It would indeed be a feat of parochialism
to which even common-sense should be unequal
to maintain that only that kind of world which
is perceived by the sense organs of human bodies
heated to a temperature of 98·4 is real. Even a counting of heads discredits it ; most organisms, after all,
are cold blooded, and a frog's world is certainly not
ours. As with the frog's world, so with the mystic's.
Most mystics have been ascetics. Ascetic practices
are methods for inducing artificially a certain kind of
psychological and physiological condition. The condition modifies the perceiving apparatus, and the
mystics' universe is accordingly changed. Changed,
and, it may be, deepened, widened, and enriched.
For men have found that the particular kind of ab-
normality that asceticism induces is one that enables
them to perceive not only a quantitatively larger, but

a qualitatively richer world. It is to them a more exciting world because of the things it contains. Goodness, for example, and beauty, and, it may be, God.
Hence they seek to retain and continually to enjoy it.
They also try to tell us about it. On the whole, however, they have failed, not because what they have
tried to describe is not real, but because of the limitations of language. If a frog could talk English, it is
most improbable that he could make us understand
the kind of world he inhabited. And where the great
mystics who have enjoyed experiences of the greatest
significance have failed, how am I, who am no mystic
at all, but merely a philosopher—who refuses to believe that men of obvious religious genius, the saints,
the seers, and the sages who have commanded the
veneration of their fellows, are all of them either
dupes or cheats, liars or gulls—to convey an idea of
that which, as it seems to me, they have tried to tell
us ? The task is a formidable one, especially since,
not being a mystic, I cannot claim the mystic's privilege of talking nonsense in an emergency, in the hope
that some of it may mean something to somebody.
Yet, since for me the mystics hold the essential truth
of religion, I must make the attempt.

First let us take stock of the materials which our
previous discussion entitles us to use. Religion, I have
tried to show, cannot be interpreted or explained exclusively in terms of its origins. In common with
other expressions of the human spirit, it must be accounted the product of an evolutionary process. Developing from humble beginnings, it has in the process of development become more than its beginnings. Just as there is more in the human body than
in the germ cell, more in modern mathematics than
mere counting, more in modern science than superstition tinctured with curiosity, so is there more in
modern religion than the desire to propitiate the
forces of nature, to win God's good offices for the
tribe or to make him a scapegoat for its misdemean-

ours. This "more," we have agreed, is to be interpreted teleologically, in terms, that is to say, of the goal which religion may be seeking to realise and of the ultimate manifestation of the fully developed human spirit realising that goal. Thus, when we are trying to gauge its significance in the present, information about the origin and history of religion may be not only irrelevant, but misleading.

One aspect of this "more" we have identified with the disinterested desire manifested in young men and women for the improvement of human life in this world. For another, and a more important, we have agreed to look to man's relation to another world, and, we affirm, it is only in a fully developed religion that we are likely to find it. No religion is yet, it is obvious, fully developed ; it is possible, it is even probable, that man's religious development lags behind his development in other spheres, in that of science, for example, or of art. Where, then, should we look for a clue to the course which religion is to take, and to the nature of the experience which religion is likely to bestow, if it is not to the highest and most noteworthy expressions of the human spirit in other but kindred spheres ? What, then, are these ?

I can answer, but I cannot defend my answer. For we enter here the realm of values, and entering it, find ourselves committed to making judgments of value which are in the last resort acts of faith. I can recount what appear to me to be the highest and most valuable manifestations of the human spirit ; I can even construct a metaphysical system to justify my choice[1] ; but, in the last resort, I must admit the possibility that my system may be nothing but a rationalisation of my own tastes. When we draw up our lists of great names, when we assign values to the activities in virtue of which we call them great, we enter the region of personal confession.

Here, then, let me make mine. Leaving religion

[1] See my *Matter, Life, and Value*. (O.U.P. 1929.)

temporarily out of account, as the subject to be presently discussed, I consider the creation of works of art and literature, and the æsthetic appreciation of such works, together with the intellectual activity of the philosopher, the mathematician, and the scientist—when his science is pure—to be the noblest expressions of the human spirit, and I consider that in such men as Bach and Mozart, Plato and Hume, Shakespeare and Tolstoy, Swift and Shaw, it has risen to its greatest heights. My literary heroes are, it will be observed, with the possible exception of Shakespeare, all of them teachers; their bent is didactic. Castigating hypocrisy and stupidity, denouncing cruelty and vice, mocking pomp and privilege, exposing conventional morality as no morality at all, they have sought to establish a new standard of right and wrong, to indicate a new conception of conduct by which, they have urged, it was men's duty to live. In a word, they were geniuses in the sphere of morals, endowed with an original vision of goodness, which was at once subtler and more profound than that of their contemporaries, just as the great artists have been distinguished by their original vision of beauty, and the great philosophers by their original conception of truth.

Putting the point in another way, we may say that life has now evolved at a stage at which, in its most advanced representatives, it is intermittently aware of what, for want of a better word, we call "value." The great artist apprehends the value which we call beauty; the sage and the moralist the value which we call goodness. Finding themselves, for reasons already given, unable to describe in language the nature of this world of value into which they have insight, they represent it as best they can in the medium most appropriate to them. The artist incarnates beauty in paint, or sound, or stone; the sage seeks to manifest goodness in the conduct of his daily life, and to lay down principles and maxims by following which others may do the same.

And just as the artist "creates"[1] a beauty of which he is unable to give any account, and the great teacher a goodness which he is unable to describe, so we who are not great artists or moralists, coming into contact with the works of the former and the lives and teaching of the latter, and apprehending the beauty which the artist and the goodness which the sage have somehow made manifest, are stirred and exalted, and are moved to declare, while the fit is on us, that art is the greatest thing in the world, or that the path which has been pointed out to us is the road to salvation and to follow it the only right way to living. Yet we cannot tell why the symphony is beautiful, any more than we can tell why the way of life is righteous. And, if pressed by another to give reasons for our appreciation of the one or the obligation which we feel to follow the other, we are at a loss to explain our excitement or to defend the judgments which it has led us to make. That, condemning or approving works of art, we are unable when taxed to justify our judgments is notorious ; we know what we like, we say irritably, and are content to leave it at that. The more sophisticated of us, it is true, talk of rhythm and metre, of harmony and counterpoint, of colour masses and perspective, of diminished sevenths and tonal effects ; we invent, in fact, the language of art criticism, which may be described as an elaborate device for camouflaging the fact that we are merely reiterating "that we know what we like."

As with beauty, so also with goodness ! We may adduce a variety of reasons why we applaud the practice of, for example, virtue ; that it promotes happiness, that it enables men to live comfortably in society, that it is advantageous to us personally, or that it qualifies the virtuous man for a place in heaven ; but these are, after all, merely descriptions more or less accurate of

[1] I put the word in inverted commas to indicate that it is being used loosely. As will presently appear, the function of the artist is, in my view, one of discovery rather than of creation.

some of the possible consequences of acting rightly ;
they are not the reasons why we admire right conduct. Hygiene promotes happiness ; an effective
police force enables men to live comfortably in
society ; gullibility in our friends is advantageous to
us personally ; and the judicious endowment of the
wings of hospitals is supposed to qualify men for
heaven. Yet we do not feel for these things the same
kind of respect as that which is aroused in us by the
practice of disinterested goodness.

Such descriptions are merely devices to disguise
from those who pride themselves on being reasonable
beings that they are totally unable to give reasons for
some of their strongest sentiments. Savages, who do
not share our wish to be thought reasonable, dispense
with them ; they venerate the good man, but are
without ethical theories. We are deeply moved by
"value" both in art and conduct, when it is made
plain to us ; our sentiments are, moreover, such as we
conceive to be a credit to us and wish to have repeated. Yet we are unable to say why it is that we
have them or to explain their significance to those
who do not. But we feel that those who do not in any
degree, however slight, share our sentiments, who
are blind and deaf to beauty in art, and unmoved by
nobility of character, are lacking in some faculty
which all adult human beings possess in so far as
they are adult and human, and that they are to that
extent not completely men and women.

But what has this to do with religion ? Precisely
this, that the apprehension of what I have called value,
not as attaching in the form of beauty to pictures or
music, or in the form of goodness to character and
conduct, but generally to the world as a whole, is in
my view the distinguishing characteristic of the religious consciousness. If we consider the state of mind
of people who are manifestly what we call religious,
we find that it involves an appreciation of something
as valuable. If we proceed further, and examine

the religious consciousness in its highest manifestation in the saint and the mystic, we find that it
always contains an element of worship, of worship
felt for the universe as a whole. This worship is an
appreciation of value ; it is or involves the feeling that
the universe is or contains an element of supreme
value which is at once the source and the sum of all
the other things which are recognised as valuable. To
this element of value the human mind naturally re-
sponds ; it excites adoration because it is felt to be
good ; it evokes worship because of its worth-ship.
Hence the religious attitude of mind is one which
contains an implicit recognition of the worth-whileness of things as a whole, not of pictures or music, of
conduct or character or truth, but of the universe
itself. And just as æsthetic experience is to be interpreted as our perception of the value called beauty as
manifested in pictures, or music, or natural scenery,
and our feeling of the supreme worth-whileness of
certain actions and characters is to be interpreted as
the recognition by the moral consciousness of the
value called goodness, so it is in mystical experience
that man has the clearest intimation of the value of the
universe considered as a whole.

I am brought here within measurable distance of the
confines of philosophy, and cannot proceed further
without trespassing beyond them. For I find that I
cannot indicate what I conceive to be the probable
future development of religion without setting forth
the particular view of the nature of the universe, of the
purpose of evolution and of the status and significance
of human life within the evolutionary process which
renders such a development probable if not inevitable. All this belongs to metaphysics, and is clearly
inappropriate in a book of this kind. I have endeavoured to expound the view in question elsewhere,
and to give the reasons for it.[1] Here I must content

[1] See *Matter, Life, and Value,* by the same author. (O.U.P.,
1929.)

myself with briefly indicating the conception of the universe as a whole to which it points, and ask the reader to take on trust the considerations on which it is based.

Life, then, I think of as an instinctive thrust or urge appearing initially in an alien environment, a dead world of chaos and blankness and matter. Life is purposive, but its purpose is at first latent, and only rises into consciousness in the course of life's evolution and development. Life evolves and develops by infusing itself into the material universe, which breaks it up, as a stream is broken by a line of rocks that lie athwart its course, into an infinity of separate living units. A living unit or organism is thus an isolated current of a vast stream or reservoir of life, temporarily incarnated in the material medium which it animates.

The living organism so formed, spurred to effort and endeavour by the limitations imposed on it by its material environment, evolves and develops, achieving new powers of skill and knowledge and understanding, and endowing itself with richer and more varied faculties. At death the individual current is merged again in the main reservoir of life, bringing with it the equipment of knowledge, skill, and faculty which in the course of its existence as an individual it has acquired. Thus the stream of life as a whole is being continuously enriched with the acquisitions which its individual units bring to it. As a result it emerges in each successive generation at a slightly higher level than before, the acquisition of knowledge and skill won by the efforts of the parents appearing in the children as an endowment of innate faculties. Thus each generation rises on the shoulders of the last, while life as a whole develops and evolves exhibiting a greater capacity for feeling, a greater power of intellect, a more subtle and penetrating faculty of insight and intuition at each level of evolutionary progress which is successively achieved.

In the course of its development life achieves the faculty of consciousness, and comes at last to a knowledge of the fact, and a glimmering of the purpose, of its evolution. It is in terms of this consciousness of purpose, this vague intimation of a goal, which is now for the first time beginning to be felt, that those expressions of the human spirit with which in this chapter I am concerned are to be interpreted. The apprehension of the goal is at once their cause and their explanation. For, in addition to the world of matter in which life appears and evolves, there is, as I conceive, a world of value to a knowledge of which life aspires. The world of value is neither mental nor material ; it is permanent, perfect, changeless, and it is in some sense the goal of the evolutionary process upon which life is engaged. It is only during the past three thousand years, an infinitesimal fraction of evolutionary time, that the existence of this world has come for the first time to be dimly realised. But, though we have assurance of its existence, we can give but the barest account of its features. It contains beauty, certainly, and goodness, and possibly truth ; and in addition to these or, perhaps as their sum, an element which mankind has come to know as deity. The awareness of this world comes to us at first in fleeting and uncertain intimations ; it is the source of our feeling for works of art, wherein we apprehend its images made by the artist in the medium of the material world, of our feeling of duty and moral obligation, or, rather, of that part of it which evades description in terms of its origin in tribal fears and of its history in social observance, and of the sense of reverence and worship which is the essence of the mystical consciousness. Our apprehension of the world of value is an evolved faculty, the latest that life has succeeded in acquiring, and it is at present the most uncertain, as it is the most precious, aspect of our consciousness. The experience of beauty in painting or music is the form in which this apprehension is most commonly vouchsafed to us. Bona fide ethical conduct and the recognition and appreciation of such conduct are widespread but intermittent and are easily obscured by passion and self-interest. Bona fide religious experience is perhaps the rarest of all. Nevertheless, it exists ; as life evolves it should grow commoner, and it is at once our duty and our pleasure to enlarge, as far as in us lies, our capacity for such experience. Widening and deepening our appreciation of value, we further the process of evolution, for the object of life's evolution, as I conceive it, is to free itself entirely from the world of matter, and to come to rest, in full, perfect, and untrammelled contemplation of the world of value.

Life is like a chrysalis, encased in the hard trappings of an alien sheath ; one day it will emerge, and, warmed by the sun of pure Being, will come to rest in that contemplation of value which mystics have called the vision of God. Meanwhile, as at all levels of evolution, there are "sports," precocious children of life on the spiritual plane, in whom the future development of the species is foreshadowed and anticipated. There are the mystics who achieve in sudden flashes of illumination that vision of the world of value which will one day, if evolution goes aright, be the privilege of all things that are living. It is from them that we derive our knowledge of the world of value, for they alone have had first-hand evidence that it exists. Were it not for the mystics, religion and all that it implies could be completely and satisfactorily interpreted in terms of its origins on the subjectivist lines that I traced in chapter vii. But, given the fact of mystical experience, we are enabled to recognise in it the developed form of that vague feeling of awe and reverence, that half-unwitting response to the universe as something worshipful, that in the ordinary man does duty as the religious sense.

Hence religion, for the developed modern consciousness, may be described as a vague and uncertain intimation of value in the universe, an intimation that is accompanied by an emotion of reverence and awed worship. This intimation logically involves, and in practice includes, the conviction that life is purposive, in the sense that it is trying to develop a clearer and fuller apprehension of what is now but imperfectly felt, and, for some of us, a recognition of the fact that in the mystic this clearer and fuller apprehension has intermittently been achieved.

Hence the future of religion is for me one in which the experience of the mystic will become the experience of the ordinary man.

So much by way of summary. Let us see to what it commits us. We are committed to the view that, in addition to the everyday material world in which we live and move and evolve, the world of struggle and change and imperfection, there is another world—permanent, perfect, and changeless. Life evolves to a fuller and more continuous knowledge of this world. To its existence, and to the hold which it already begins to exercise over men's imaginations, are to be attributed the significance we attach to beauty, the admiration we feel for moral goodness, and the sense of awe, of reverence, and of worship which the saints and mystics have called the awareness of God. What follows ?

First that beauty is a non-human, absolute value, which may be discerned and apprehended by man, which may even be copied by him, but which cannot be created by him. This is not the place for a discussion of æsthetics, and I cannot here defend this highly controversial statement.[1] But it may not be out of place to mention what has always seemed to me the most striking fact about our appreciation of art, a fact for which any theory of æsthetics must make provision. Strike a dozen notes at random on the piano, and you will evoke a series of vibrations in the atmo-

---

[1] I have tried to do it elsewhere. See my *Matter, Life, and Value*, chap. vi.

N R

sphere, completely describable in terms of physics, which in their turn produce a series of reactions in the brain, which are theoretically completely describable in terms of physiology. Arrange the same notes in such a way that they form the statement of a Bach fugue, and they can thrill you to ecstasy. And no description in terms of physics or physiology, of etheric waves or processes in the cochlea, can give the remotest explanation of the difference between the two effects, or of why there should be a difference. Yet here assuredly is something that requires an explanation.

And one explanation, perhaps the most satisfactory, may be that the arrangement of notes in the fugue has caught the likeness of some pattern belonging to the world of value, so that in virtue of the likeness the music becomes a window through which we glimpse that world. Thus the artist plays the part of a midwife, bringing to birth the forms and shapes of the world of value in the material media of sound and paint and stone. Art, then, has no concern with this world except in so far as it can be used as a medium for the representation of another one. Art is imitative, but it imitates not the sounds and objects of the material world, but the structure of the reality that lies behind it.

Taking this view, we shall see in much modern art, and indeed in most of the pictorial art that has succeeded the Renaissance, a misconception of art's proper function. The Renaissance ushered in an age of humanism. The human spirit embarked on a voyage of adventure, acquired a new culture and scholarship, won a mastery over nature, and found a key to unlock the secrets of the material universe. For a time nothing seemed too difficult for its attempting, nothing too high for its achieving. As the scroll of humanity's triumphs lengthened and grew more splendid, there was a glorification of the spirit that achieved them. The human spirit was represented as something of supreme importance. It was at once

the standard and criterion of value and the centre of
the universe ; so much so, indeed, that the rest of the
universe came to be regarded as only there for the
purpose of putting the human spirit in its centre.
Any suggestion of a non-human, perfect, and permanent world, to a knowledge of which the living and
the vital might aspire, but with which it could never
be identified, was denounced as treachery to the in-
finitely hopeful prospects of the human race. The
doctrine of evolution has lent countenance to this
view, suggesting that the evolving world of living
organisms is the only kind of world that exists, with
the result that our notions of value tend to identify it
with some future stage of the same process as that of
which we ourselves form part.

As it is only too obvious that no human thing here
and now *is* perfect, we place perfection at some distance, preferably infinite, along the road which we
are following. This is the essence of Romanticism in
literature, of Naturalism in ethics, and of Utopianism
in the social sciences. In literature we envisage an
impossible perfection in the ultimate development of
love between the sexes ; in ethics we conceive the
possibility of the immediate or gradual achievement
of perfection by the abolition of disciplines and restraints ; and in the social sciences by the removal of
certain specific inequalities and abuses.

It is part of the same tendency that in art we should
come to identify the beautiful with the objects of this
world in which we pass our everyday lives—that is to
say, with the natural, the vital, and above all the human. Hence post-Renaissance art is essentially representative in that it aims at giving as perfect a reproduction as possible of natural, living forms. This is to
degrade art to the level of photography. The function
of art, if I am right, is to give us the vision of another
world, not to photograph this one, and such a vision
is not to be achieved by a faithful representation of
the faces and forms that make our daily environ-

ment. Before the Renaissance, this, which now seems a heresy, was taken for granted. Realising the insignificance of the human spirit in the vast immensity of the universe, unimpressed with the importance of themselves and their fellows, imbued in fact with the sense of sin, it did not occur to the men of the pre-Renaissance civilisations to identify perfection with the future improvement of themselves. For them there was another world, more real because more perfect than this one, before which and before the God who inhabited it they abased themselves in humility and awe. And so their art is imbued with a radically different conception of the nature of beauty, and the significance of the material objects in which it is manifested.

The broad difference between pre- and post-Renaissance pictorial art may be described by saying, that, while post-Renaissance art is a "vital" art in that it takes and endeavours to communicate a delight in human and natural forms, pre-Renaissance art is the exact contrary to this. There is, for example, in Byzantine pictures and mosaics no figure or shape that is either natural or vital, nor is the pleasure we obtain from them a pleasure in the reproduction of natural objects or of human figures. There is rather a neglect of the appearances of things and a preoccupation with the formal qualities of lines and shapes. There is, further, a definite impatience with whatever in the appearance of living organisms and of natural objects fails to exhibit such lines and shapes in the purity of their abstract form. This impatience is the expression of a fundamental indifference to the trivial and accidental characteristics of living matter, and a searching after an austerity, a rigidity, a *perfection* which vital things can never have. We cannot suppose that the mason who carved the face of an archaic figure did not possess the skill to separate the arms and legs from the body, or that the conventional forms of Egyptian monumental sculpture spring from an incapacity to

represent real ones. We can only conclude that these
deficiencies in realism reflect a particular kind of interest, and that in Egyptian, Indian, and Byzantine
art, where everything tends to be hard and geo-
metrical, the representation of the human body is
often distorted to fit into a framework of stiff lines
and cubical shapes because the artist was interested
in the human body not for its own sake, but only in so
far as it exemplifies lines and shapes, Man, in short,
is subordinated in pre-Renaissance art to certain non-
human absolute values ; his form is never presented
intact, but distorted and mutilated in order that it
may be made to fit into certain abstract patterns
which arouse æsthetic emotion.

This attitude to natural objects reflects, in my view,
a right conception of art. It implies that the significance of a work of art depends upon the extent to
which the artist has succeeded in representing in it
the beauty which, in virtue of his special insight, he
has apprehended in the world of value. It is only on
some supposition of this kind—a supposition which
presupposes the existence of an order of being other
than that with which in daily life we are normally
acquainted—that the peculiar effect and appeal of art
can be explained. It follows that art is meaningless in
the sense that the peculiar quality in which its appeal
resides, and to which its effect upon men's minds is
due, has no meaning in relation to the things of this
world, and cannot be explained in terms of the language appropriate to the things of this world. It is for
this reason that in the last resort we are unable to say
why we like a work of art, what it is that provokes our
admiration, or what we mean by calling it beautiful.
Strictly speaking, art criticism should not exist.

Similarly with goodness. We all of us recognise that
certain actions ought to be done, and that certain
characters have what we call ethical value. Why ?
Various rational explanations are given. It is said, for
example, that we ought to perform a certain action

because it will promote the greatest happiness of the greatest number, or that we approve of a good character because it is sociably valuable. But if these and similar explanations are correct, we ought to do what is right and we approve of what is good not because what is right and what is good are valuable in themselves, but for the sake of their consequences, because, presumably, their consequences are valuable. It follows that any theory which asserts that the justification for ethical conduct lies not in the conduct itself, but in its results, is not, as it at first sight appears to be, a theory about what is good or right at all, but about the expected consequences of what is good or right, such consequences as, for example, in the cases cited, happiness or social utility ; and it is about these consequences that it affirms that they are valuable. Ethics, if such theories are correct, appeals not to our sense of value, but to our sense of prudence.

That this is so can be seen by considering the character of the appeal made by the ordinary moral maxim. "Honesty," we affirm, "is the best policy," and, affirming it, imply that a sufficient cause for acting honestly is not to be found in honesty itself. We approve honesty, it seems, not for its own sake, but for the sake of the consequences in the shape of serenity, wealth, and social reputation which attend its habitual practice. Or, again, we say, "God loves an upright man," implying that we ought to be upright not because of a considered preference for rectitude, but because by being upright we shall win God's favour. All religions have taken care to paint the respective consequences of winning God's favour and arousing his anger in the liveliest colours, the result being to transfer to the next world the incentive to moral conduct which "honesty is the best policy" supplies for this one.

Now goodness—it is clear—which is valued for the sake of its results is not valued for itself at all. Yet

directly we begin to rationalise about ethics, to analyse goodness, to say why we ought to do what is
good, or to explain what we mean by being good, we
find that what we are in fact describing is either the
incentive to be good or the results of being good ;
we are not, that is to say, talking about goodness itself
at all. A rational account of goodness could only be
given in terms of its results or its causes. To give
reasons why we should be good would imply that we
should be good because of the potency of the reasons
we have advanced, or, in other words, because of
something other than goodness. In the majority of
cases, this something other than goodness which is
advanced as a reason why we should be good turns
out on analysis to be the results or consequences of
being good ; reasons given for being good are that it
pays, that it will make us happy, or that God or other
people like it.

But if no rational account can be given of goodness,
if goodness itself is in essence non-rational, it follows
that it is not possible to defend goodness to a moral
sceptic, or to persuade a man who feels no moral inclination either to be good or to want to be good, by
advancing reasons why he should pursue goodness.
This conclusion seems to be convincingly borne out
by the experience of those who have engaged in
preaching or moral exhortation. Nothing, indeed, is
more remarkable in ethics than the failure of the
method of direct moral exhortation to produce effective results. For two thousand years teachers and
preachers have striven, by inculcating the principles
and precepts of Christianity, to mould men's characters and to improve their conduct ; yet we still have
our prisons, our judges, and our wars, and it remains
to-day, as it has done for two thousand years past, an
arguable question whether men are better or worse
than they were before Christianity was introduced.

It seems to follow that in the last resort goodness,
like beauty, is indefinable, and indefinable because it

is essentially unreasonable. We can recognise that certain actions are right and certain characters are good, just as we recognise that certain smells are pleasant and others unpleasant, and that is all that there is to be said about it. That this is so can be proved by five minutes' argument on any moral issue. Let us suppose that we are endeavouring to persuade a man to act in a way which we intuitively perceive to be right. We bring forward, in the first instance, arguments in support of the course advocated based on utilitarian considerations : "Do this," we say, "if you wish to prosper." "Do this, because so and so will expect it," or "Do this, if you don't want to be thought a blackguard" ; thus, by appeals addressed to his prudence or his fear, we seek to persuade him to the right course. Let us suppose, further, that these appeals fail, and fail because he attaches a different weight to the considerations brought forward from that which we have been inclined to place upon them, that, in short, he takes a different view of his interests and of what is best calculated to advance them. We are thrown back on our last line of attack ; we bring up our ethical reserves. "Do this," we say, "because it is the only decent thing to do. Do it because it is right." If this appeal, too, proves fruitless, what more can we say ? Our plea may, of course, be rejected on the ground that, although it is agreed that what we advocate ought to be done, the sacrifice involved is greater than our friend finds himself able to make. In this case the difference between us is not primarily an ethical one, and does not, therefore, affect the issue I wish to raise. But let us suppose that our friend simply fails to recognise the moral obligation that we seek to invoke ; that he does not share our view that the action indicated is the only decent thing to do, that he does not, in other words, feel that the contrary action is wrong. We can bring no further argument in support of our contention ; we can appeal only to an ultimate and unanalysable intuition, and,

since it is an intuition which *ex hypothesi* he does not
share, the appeal falls on deaf ears. If he does not see
that the action in question ought to be performed, we
can only abandon the hope of influencing him in the
regretful conviction that what our friend lacks is a
moral sense.

The conclusion is that the man with moral insight
apprehends certain values—the value of goodness for
example, and its manifestation in conduct and character—which the man without it does not, just as the
man of æsthetic sensibility recognises certain other
values—the nature of beauty and its manifestation in
shapes and sounds and lines—which the man without
it does not. And, similarly, the man of religious insight apprehends certain values which the man without it does not. What values ? We can only answer,
the values which are what we call divine. But what do
we mean by values which are divine ? Certainly not
a personal, semi-human Creator. For the view I am
putting forward involves the conception of deity not
as the creator of this world, but as the occupant of
another, not as the source and origin of life, but as the
goal and end of its pilgrimage. To conceive of God as
the source of all that is, and therefore as the principle
to which we ourselves owe our being, is to raise the
insoluble problems considered in chapter vi. A perfect God could not, we said, feel the need to create,
a benevolent God made accountable for the occurrence of pain and evil, or an omnipotent God saddled
with the responsibility of deceiving his creatures.

The force of these considerations is, to my mind,
overwhelming. To acknowledge them is to acknowledge the impossibility of a God who is conceived as
permanent and perfect owning any relation with a
world which is changing and imperfect, with the
changing and imperfect living beings that inhabit it,
or with the principle of life that animates them. Like
goodness and beauty, He must be a non-human
value, whose significance consists in His very unlike-

ness to the life that aspires to Him. He may be known
by life, and, as life evolves and develops, he may be
known increasingly, the first fleeting intimations of
the saints and mystics reaching their consummation
in the continuous joy of unclouded contemplation.
But God Himself is unaffected by such contemplation, and, though to achieve it may be the end and
purpose of life's evolution, He is unaware of the
movement of life towards Him. Nor can life enter into
communion with Him. God, it is obvious, if He is to be
an object worthy of our adoration, must be kept un-
spotted from the world that adores Him. To suppose
that the mystic can enter into communion with Him
is to suppose Him infected with the frailties and imperfections of the mystic ; to suppose that the saint
can become one with Him is to suppose that He can
become one with the saint. But, I repeat, the permanent and perfect cannot be continuous with the imperfect and the changing ; nor could it, without
ceasing to be itself, enter into communion with the
imperfect and the changing. For this reason, though
the religious consciousness may hope to know God,
the religious man cannot aspire to become one with
that which he knows.

That a Being so conceived exists the mystics have
borne unanimous testimony. Either we are to write
off this testimony as the idle babbling of men beside
themselves with solitude and fasting, or we must accept it as evidence of a something beyond, into which
the vision of the mystic has penetrated. In this light I
for one am prepared to regard it. Mystical insight, if
I am right, is not just an exciting, subjective feeling,
subjective in the sense in which toothache is subjective, but an awareness of an object and a feeling of
reverence and exaltation in the presence of that object. Mystical experience has, no doubt, its origin in
the primitive emotions of man's past ; it is the fruit
of training both of mind and body, and is the outcome of vigorous mental and spiritual activity. Self-

discipline, both intellectual and physical, and a continued striving after right living and purity of motive, prepare the soul for its illumination. But the illumination itself is a thing apart, transcending the origins from which it arose, and divorced from the preparation of mind and spirit which has led up to it. The origin of the mystical consciousness in primitive emotion, the preparatory training, moral and spiritual, of the soul are of this world ; but the illumination itself is a direct vision into another. It is the window, the clearest as yet, through which man has glimpsed reality, the avenue of the soul's approach to God.

To write of this experience is difficult for one who has not enjoyed it. Yet it is, in my view, the highest development of the religious consciousness which life has yet achieved, and in a book which attempts to forecast the future development of religion some account, however vague, must be given of its nature. Its object, that *of* which it is the vision, must, if I am right, remain unknown to us. The world which mystics contemplate is revealed only to the mystics ; but of the character of the experience itself we may obtain some inkling, by considering its closest analogue in that of the ordinary man—namely, that intimation of the world of value which comes to us in æsthetic experience.

What, then, are the characteristics of intense æsthetic experience ? There are, I think, two. In the first place it brings with it a sense of freedom and release ; in the second, it is fleeting and evanescent. As instruments of evolution, we are in our day-to-day existence mere channels through which flows restlessly and unceasingly the current of life. We are a surge of impulses, a battlefield of desires, over which we can only at length and after a lifetime of setback and of struggle obtain a degree of mastery through the achievement of a self-discipline, which is itself the outcome of desire made rational. Wishing, fearing, craving, hoping, willing, we may never, except in the rare moments of æsthetic enjoyment, be at rest. We must be for ever doing and stirring, improving and making better, meddling and changing. It is one of the paradoxes of our nature that we cannot even love a thing without seeking to change it, and by changing to make it other than what we love. The greatest lovers of mankind have been those who have spent their lives in the endeavour to save mankind ; and, since they have always insisted that mankind could not be saved except it repented, to save man was to alter him. A man cannot love a woman without seeking to mould her nearer to his heart's desire, or a child without trying to form it upon himself. We cannot love the countryside without pruning and clipping, smartening and tidying, making meaningful and useful what has achieved beauty by haphazard, and imposing order upon the sweet disorder of nature. We cannot love a tree even, or a stone, but sooner or later we must be pruning the tree or chipping a piece off the stone. We do these things because of the overmastering impulsion of our wills ; yet were it not for our wills we should cease to be. Thus, for so long as we live, we must conform to the bidding of the life within us, so that, however we love and whatever we love, it can be for a few moments only, and to buy off our will for these moments we have to relinquish what we love to it, to change and alter as it needs must for the rest of our lives.

This, then, is the law of our being as units of the stream of life, that we should be for ever changing ourselves, and seeking to change the world around us. But this law, which is the law of life as evolving to an end, is not the law of life which has achieved the end. And so there is even now an exception to the law, in virtue of which we partake, if only for a moment, of the rest and freedom which it is the object of life to win permanently and to win for everything that is living. In the appreciation of music and of pictures

we get a momentary and fleeting glimpse of the nature of that reality to a full knowledge of which the
movement of life is progressing. For that moment,
and for so long as the glimpse persists, we realise in
anticipation and almost, as it were, illicitly, the nature
of the end. We are, if I may so put it, for the moment
there, just as a traveller may obtain a fleeting glimpse
of a distant country from a height reached on the way,
and cease for a space from his journey to enjoy the
view. And since we are for the moment *there*, we experience while the moment lasts that sense of liberation from the drive of life, which has been noted as
one of the special characteristics of æsthetic experience. We who are part and parcel of the evolutionary
stream stand for the time outside and above the
stream, and are permitted for a moment to be withdrawn from the thrust and play of impulse and desire,
which are our natural attributes as evolutionary tools.
For so long as we enjoy the vision of the end, life lets
us alone. We feel neither need nor want, and, losing
ourselves in contemplation of the reality beyond us,
we become for the moment selfless.

But if, in æsthetic experience, we are like travellers,
resting on our journey and refreshing ourselves with
a view of the goal to which our steps are directed, we
may not rest for long. The Life Force has created us
for a purpose, and it cannot afford to have us dallying by the roadside. Indulgence in æsthetic experience is, from the point of view of the Life Force, a
form of idling, a playing truant when we should be
at school. "Biologically speaking," says Mr. Roger
Fry, "art is a blasphemy. We were given our eyes
to see things and not to look at them."[1] Thus life
takes care that at an early age we shall attain to a considerable ignorance of the visual appearance of objects. We see and we are meant to see only so much of
them as serves the purpose of living. To see them
whole and to see them round as the artist does, to see

[1] Fry, *Vision and Design*, chap. iv., p. 47.

them, above all, as combinations of significant forms,
is a kind of seeing for which those who are preoccu-
pied with the business of living cannot afford the
energy or the time.

We are all familiar, to take the matter at its lowest,
with the limitations of the sense of smell. Agreeable
odours please us only fitfully ; the sensation comes as
a surprise, a pleasing shock, and is quickly gone. If
we attempt to hold it by deliberately smelling a frag-
rant flower, we begin to have a sense of failure as
though we had exhausted the pleasure, keen as it was
a moment ago. For this failure to retain there is no
doubt a physiological basis ; a nerve is tired and requires an interval of rest before it can be freshly stimulated. But for me the distinction between psychological and physiological occurrences in the last resort
breaks down. Each type of occurrence resolves itself
into a form of awareness, and so, when we turn to
what passes for a more spiritual because more developed faculty and consider the sense of sight, we find,
though in a less marked degree, the same evanescence
in æsthetic pleasure. We look long and steadily at a
thing to know it, and the longer and more fixedly we
look, the better, if it engages the reasoning faculties ;
but our æsthetic pleasure cannot be increased or retained in this way. To gaze fixedly at the most beautiful object in nature or art does but diminish the
pleasure. Practically it ceases to be beautiful, and
only recovers the first effect after we have given ourselves an interval of rest. If we would get the keenest
visual pleasure we must look, merely glancing as it
were, and look again, and then again, receiving at in-
tervals the image in the brain even as we receive the
perfume of a flower ; and the image is all the brighter
for coming intermittently.

That it should be at once unexpected and intermittent is characteristic of our pleasure in the beautiful in whatever form it is presented. Beauty always
takes us as it were by surprise, whether it comes to us

as a sudden view of a landscape, as a harmony of
shape and line, or it may be as music heard by chance
from an open window in the street. Nor is the reason
far to seek. Æsthetic apprehension is unconditioned
by considerations of space and time, and unrelated to
the purposes of life ; for this reason we are not
allowed to indulge it overmuch. And so, before we
are even fully assured that the vision of beauty is ours,
the Life Force catches us up and thrusts us back into
the whirlpool of want and need, of striving, loving,
and fearing which is life. And this no doubt is the
reason for the fleeting and ephemeral nature of even
the most lasting æsthetic experience ; to this it owes
its unsatisfactory and tantalising character. There is
no sky in June so blue that it does not point forward
to a bluer ; no sunset so beautiful that it does not
awaken the thought of a greater beauty. The soul is at
once gladdened and disappointed. The veil is lifted
so quickly that we have scarcely time to know that it
has gone before it has fallen again. But during the
moment of lifting we get a vision of a something behind and beyond, which passes before it is clearly
seen, and which in passing leaves behind a feeling of
indefinable longing and regret.

That these are the characteristics of intense æsthetic
experience is, I think, undeniable, and, if I am right in
regarding mysticism as conveying a direct view of a
world which in art we approach by roundabout ways,
they may be conceived to be in an even greater degree
the characteristics of mystical experience. The vision
of that to which the mystic gives the name of God
has, then, these two qualities ; it brings a sense of
freedom and selflessness, but it is also fleeting and uncertain. So much we may, I think, fairly affirm. Yet
of the characteristics of the object revealed, of the God
whom mystics enjoy, we can give no account. For
mysticism, as I pointed out at the beginning, is from
its very nature debarred from giving an account of itself. In affirming that mystical experience is at once

exalting and exciting, and that it brings a feeling of emancipation from self, the mystics are unanimous ; but they have not succeeded in conveying its content. The God of whom they speak may be nothing but a generalised name for the world of value, a symbol to denote the element of perfection and permanence in the universe. He may be beauty and goodness and truth taken in sum, or these may be but partial aspects of Him, different facets of His nature. He may, in other words, be all the elements of value taken together, or a unity of which they are but partial revelations. We cannot tell. All that we are entitled to say is that deeper than the complex of feelings which has gone to the making of religion, the humility and reverence, the sense of an obligation to mankind, the feeling of imperativeness and acting under orders which has traditionally been interpreted as divine inspiration, lies the sense of a mystery half revealed, of a hidden beauty and glory, of a transfiguring vision in which common things lose their solid importance, and become a thin veil behind which the ultimate reality of the universe is dimly seen. It is this sense which has been the source of all that is noblest in religion in the past, and which, if religion is to survive, it must seek to refine and to extend in the future.

Our argument may be summarised as follows : (i.) Art and morals can only be adequately explained on the assumption that in æsthetic and ethical experience we are brought into direct touch with a world of value. (ii.) In mystical experience man has achieved his most direct and continuous vision of this world. (iii.) As life evolves the vision becomes clearer and the insight deeper. (iv.) Religion, while assuring us of the existence of this world, should teach that way of life by means of which we may be brought to a fuller and more continuous knowledge of it. It is the function of religion, in other words, to help forward the process of evolution.

Chapter XI

THE FUTURE OF RELIGION

Or

THE FUTURE OF RELIGION

Rejection of a creed is not inconsistent with being possessed by a living belief.[1]

In this concluding chapter I want to answer as briefly as I can the question with which I began this book : What are the conditions which a religion which is to survive in the modern world must satisfy ? The answer has already been implied in the discussions of the two previous chapters, and I have only to bring to a focus and to summarise the conclusions which have been reached.

The considerations which are relevant to an estimate of the prospects of religion are of two kinds, positive and negative. There are the conditions which religion must fulfil and the anachronisms from which religion must abstain. I will take the negative ones first.

I. What things, then, must a religion which is to survive not do ?

(*a*) It must not teach beliefs about the nature of the physical universe which science has shown to be false.

(*b*) With regard to the non-physical universe, it must not teach as absolute truths dogmas which cannot be known to be either true or false, but which there is no reason to think true.

Condition (*a*) rules out all religions of the Fundamentalist type. For these, unless civilisation is to collapse and the world to relapse into savagery, there can be no future. Whatever, on general grounds, may be the prospects of such a relapse, the vogue of Fundamentalism in the form in which it has broken out in the United States should, in any event, be short lived.

[1] Professor Eddington, lecturing to the Society of Friends, May 1929.

In this connection it is not without significance that an authoritative rebuff should have recently been delivered to His more injudicious supporters by the very Being whom their unsolicited testimony has so palpably embarrassed. I read that on the day on which Kentucky approved by a referendum a law to prohibit any reference to evolution in its schools, a baby was born in Knoxville, Tennessee, with a tail seven inches long.[1] This Providential intervention by the principal in an acrimonious dispute seems to be intended to convey the plainest possible hint in the most tactful possible way.

The hint, I gather, is on the whole being taken. Despite the strength of the old-fashioned Fundamentalists who are entrenched in the southern and western States, Modernism is making a steady and irresistible advance in the religious life of the United States. If I may for the last time invoke the assistance of one of those statistical investigations by means of which Americans endeavour to find out what each other thinks, I should like to quote some figures prepared by the Rev. G. H. Betts, Professor of Religious Education in the North Western Modernist University, tabulating answers by 500 Protestant clergymen and 200 students in theological seminaries.

No less than 94 per cent. of the students believed that the theory of evolution is consistent with the idea of God as a creator, and 61 per cent. of the ministers thought the same. Only 28 per cent. of the ministers believed in hell as an actual place or locality, and 11 per cent. of the students. Less than half of the ministers (47 per cent.) believed that the Creation occurred in the manner and at the time recorded in Genesis. The discovery that in the United States, and apparently in the less civilised parts of the United States, more than half the clergymen questioned believe that

[1] The tail, I gather, has been removed and sent to the John Hopkins University at Baltimore, where it will be kept to show that a referendum, though it may deny, cannot evade, the truth.

the first book of the Bible is untrue is as gratifying as it is surprising.

Fundamentalism, it seems clear, is on the wane.

Condition (*b*) is not less important. Religions have included in the past a definite set of dogmas with regard to such matters as the purpose of existence and the government of the universe, in which those who professed the religion were required to believe. The dogmas were unsupported by evidence, could not be verified by experience, and related to matters with regard to which the truth was unobtainable. The Christian religion has been particularly rich in dogmas of this kind. For example, Jesus's relation to God and to the Holy Ghost has been expounded in a number of highly complex theories, and Unitarians and Nestorians, Eutychians, Aryans, and Monophysites have maintained with considerable emphasis divergent views, which have been the occasion of interminable disputes. These views were put forward not as hypotheses which were more or less probable, but as absolute truths, the acceptance of which was claimed by their adherents as indispensable to salvation. The view which finally prevailed finds expression in that monument of lucidity the Athanasian creed, and this, presumably, holds the field to-day.

Now, it is just possible that one of these views may be true ; but it cannot be known to be so. If it be asserted that its truth is revealed to insight, then it may be authoritative for the elect to whom the insight has been vouchsafed ; but it cannot claim authority over those to whom it has not. The unofficial sentiments on the matter of the average devout Christian to-day are presumably somewhat as follow : "I believe in God and try to live like Jesus, but I do not know exactly what the relation between them is, nor do I very much care." To insist that he must know, and must care, is either to drive him away from the Church, or to insist on his becoming a hypocrite, if he chooses to remain.

A creed for the modern mind is merely a working hypothesis. It is always possible that it may be true, and it may, therefore, be provisionally entertained until something better turns up ; but it cannot be known to be true, is probably false in certain particulars, and is not to be made a test of faith. These considerations apply not only to the obsolete creeds of the past, but to any others by which they may be superseded. A creed "in harmony with the thought of to-day," or a religion based on the discoveries of modern science, will be as dangerous as the Athanasian creed—more dangerous, in fact, for it will take more people in—if it is accepted as a statement of truth and not as a working hypothesis. For a creed in "harmony with the thought of to-day" will be out of harmony with that of to-morrow, and a religion based on the discoveries of modern science will be discredited by the discoveries of a science still more modern. But while creeds and religions which make creeds a test of faith may be discredited by science, religion in the sense described in the last chapter will remain unaffected. Naturally, since it is concerned with something different.

It is, indeed, precisely because, in spite of doctrinaires and zealots, it has always been vaguely felt that the Church of England stood for something more than creeds, that it survives to-day. There is a tradition in this Church, a tradition supported and enriched by a long line of English clergymen (particularly country clergymen), that what a man believes is less important than the way he behaves, that an acceptance of metaphysical notions about the Trinity is less essential than an endeavour to live according to the principles of the Sermon on the Mount, that the custom of baptism matters more than its doctrine, and that the religious benefits which the poor man derives from the church where his fathers worshipped, and the sacred piece of turf where they lie buried, are but little dependent on a clear understanding of the Liturgy or the Sermon. As for the clergyman, an insight into men's characters becomes him better than an interest in their opinions.

In the course of this book I have had some hard things to say of the Church. It is the pleasanter to be able to record one's unstinted admiration for this type of country clergymen. It is because something of their tradition still lingers in the Church to-day that it commands the reverence and respect of many who disbelieve most of the dogmas upon which it officially insists, and is likely to survive its Nonconformist rivals with their more doctrinaire tradition. But only for a time. The religion of the future has no place for metaphysical truths that can be formulated as absolute dogmas. We know too much about the universe to-day to think that we know anything for certain. Yet the modern man's intransigeance in the matter of formulated creeds does not imply the end of religion as in the last chapter I have conceived religion. "Religion," said Professor Eddington, lecturing to the Society of Friends, "for the conscientious seeker is not all a matter of doubts and self-questioning. There is a kind of sureness which is very different from cock-sureness." I agree. But it is not the sureness which can be stated in words or finds expression in explicit beliefs.

II. On the positive side the religion of the future will have two functions to perform. The first concerns man's relation to his fellow-men, the second his relation to the universe as a whole. A religion which the modern man can take seriously must seriously address itself to the needs of the time. If the Western world paid any attention to the religion it professes, it would scrap its armies and navies, close its prisons, sack its judges, and adopt some form of economic Communism. These, no doubt, are Utopian projects, but that it should make some attack upon the major evils of our day should not be too much to ask of a religion. In so doing it would appeal to and provide expression for the political impulse which, in those who wish to help their fellows and to improve the world in which they live, is now thwarted and frustrated by the size of the modern community. The course of events since the war has seemed at times to suggest that the days of democracy may be numbered, and that the future rests with disciplined bodies of determined men and women, resolved to take hold of the affairs of society and to run them not as dominant groups have run them in the past, to promote their own interests, but in what they believe to be the interests of society as a whole. That they should be mistaken as to the nature of these interests, and should be led to devote their energies to the service of ends which are harmful, is their inevitable heritage from man's tragic past, which it should be the function of religion to replace by a new conception of what is socially valuable. To believe that one not only knows what is right, but is justified in imposing one's conception on others, is natural to the young and vigorous, and the course of history has been largely determined by the childish attempt to make others think as we think, value what we value, and behave as we behave ; inevitably, since the race itself is still in its infancy. It has been one of the chief hindrances to man's advancement that a mature and civilised outlook, and a just conception of what is valuable, has only been achieved at a time of life when the energy and will to make them effective are lacking.

It should be the business of religion to substitute for the ends that have inspired most of men's collective actions in the past—the desire for wealth or power, the fear of rivals and the wish to dictate loyalties, to determine beliefs and to prescribe conduct—the values of the mind and the spirit, and to mobilise the energies which have been hitherto used to keep back the evolution of the race to help it forward. Wells's book, *The Open Conspiracy*, is a religion in this sense,

and the religion of the future will appeal to the idealism of the young and vigorous in, proportion as it
embodies this or some similar programme of measures
recognised to be for the good, not of individuals, nor
even of nations, but of mankind.

In the second place, religion must concern itself
with man's relation to the universe as a whole. To
comfort and console man in the face of the apparent
indifference of the physical world, to assure him of
the underlying worth-whileness of things, has always
been its most important function, upon the performance of which its prospects in the future will chiefly
depend.

Bearing in mind the origins of religion in primitive
fear and need which we discussed in chapter vii., we
shall naturally expect some part of the rôle which
religion plays in the life of the modern man to be determined by these origins. Man is still clogged by the
heritage of his past, and cannot yet hope to emanci-
pate himself from the needs which it engenders. In
all of us there are vestigial elements of those primitive
emotions which first prompted the savage to make
gods in order that he might propitiate them, a sense
of helplessness before the face of nature, a feeling of
insignificance before the vastness and indifference of
the universe, and a need to find compensation for the
slights and injustices of this life in the egotistically
conceived glories of another. In our moments of
weakness these emotions revive ; to all of us comes
the need for comfort and consolation, to all of us the
desire to be important and to feel esteemed. And to
all of us, therefore, the primitive side of religion must
continue at moments, however faintly, to appeal,
strengthening and sustaining us, and giving us the
assurance, albeit illusory, of protection and guidance
in the present and welcome and consideration in the
future. Nor is religion when it comes in this guise to
be condemned, merely because some of us have outgrown it. At its best the religion of the past, as, com-

forting and strengthening, it ministered to the needs
from which it sprang, was a fine thing and brought
happiness into humble lives. It alone has had the
power to take men out of and lift them above themselves, and under its influence rough men and weary-
hearted women drank in a faith which was a rudi-
mentary culture, which linked their thoughts with the
past, lifted their imaginations above the sordid details of their own narrow lives, and suffused their
souls with the sense of a pitying, loving Presence,
sweet as summer to the houseless needy.

Such has been the rôle which religion at its best has
played in the life of the common man. For those who
have been unfitted by circumstances of training and
intelligence for this simple faith, for the educated
modern mind, at once enquiring and disillusioned,
critical of the dogmas of orthodox religion and contemptuous of the Churches, yet conscious nevertheless of a pointlessness and purposelessness in life,
which spring from a sense of spiritual deficiency, it is
clear that religion, if it is to survive, must come to
mean something more than this.

Twentieth-century man I have represented as the
victim of an unconscious need to believe. How is that
need to be satisfied ? It can be satisfied only if he can
be somehow assured of the fundamental worth-
whileness of the universe. It is the function of religion, as I conceive it, to give him this assurance. To do
this it must make him realise that the scientific account of the physical universe popular to-day, or
rather yesterday (for the most modern physics has
made the world at once less alien and more mysterious), is neither final nor exhaustive. The universe is
not a pointless, purposeless collocation of atoms ;
evolution is not a mere movement of material ; life
is not a chance passenger straying across a fundamentally alien universe ; value not a mere projection
of the human spirit upon the empty canvas of a fea-
tureless world. The *material* universe may, it is true,

be a chance aggregate of physical entities, but this
material world is moulded and infused by a spirit of
life. Moreover, it is not the only world, but behind
and beyond it is the world of value, permanent and
perfect. Our conceptions of beauty, of goodness, and
of God are not, therefore, figments of desire and
wraiths of the imagination, will-o'-the-wisps to lead
astray the fond and the foolish, but life's recognition
in us, its most advanced representatives, of the existence of this world, and acknowledgment of its compelling power.

For life is not a pointless journey, but a crusade
through the world of matter in search of the world of
value and perfection, and evolution is the process of
life's development as it seeks to equip itself for the
apprehension of that world. It rests with us, life's
most advanced representatives, to carry forward that
process still further. Hence we are not isolated units
mattering to nobody but ourselves, but participators
in an undertaking which is greater than ourselves,
and individuality is not an end in itself, but a means
to an end which transcends it.

The spiritual loneliness of the agnostic's universe reflects unfavourably upon men's lives, generating in
the individual the belief that it matters to nobody but
himself how his life is lived. Just as the size of the
modern State makes him feel that he no longer counts
as a citizen, so does the indifference of the modern
universe make him feel that he no longer counts as a
man. Hence men lose their sense of value because
value in a universe so conceived has no meaning, and
personal satisfaction comes to be regarded as the sole
criterion of what is worth while. But we have not yet
evolved at a level at which we can dispense with the
conceptions of duty and obligation, and the acknowledgment of no responsibility but to the self makes
not for freedom, but for self-imposed slavery. A life
so conceived is a tired and tiring life, slavery to the
need for individual pleasure being the most burden-

some of all the forms of servitude to which men and
women have hitherto subjected themselves. For once
we fall into the mercantilist error of judging life solely
as a commerical speculation, with pleasure on the
profit side and pain on the debit, we are bound to find
it a failure. Taken as isolated units, we are nervous
little clods of wants and ailments perpetually present-
ing our cheques for pleasure at the bank of existence,
and first indignantly and then querulously abusing
life for refusing to honour them. Like children, we
demand that our fellows shall take us at our own valu-
ation and minister to our self-importance ; and, because they refuse, we turn cynic and pessimist, con-
demn existence as a bad investment and life as a
meaningless adventure in a purposeless universe.
This is the plight of the generation now coming to
maturity, which, having successfully revolted against
authority, is finding itself increasingly disillusioned
with the results of its revolt. It has knocked the
bottom out of the spiritual universe and sent the
gods packing ; but it has still to come to terms with
the need which created them. The solicitations of
this need, thwarted and driven underground, are
responsible for much of the world weariness which,
as we saw in chapter v., is so characteristic of the
age.

Religion, as I have defined it, can rescue us from
this impasse. Intimating that the meaning of this
world must be sought outside it, it bestows, nevertheless, a meaning upon the world. Assuring us that
our highest faculties and noblest inspirations have
their origin in a world which is not known to the
senses, it invests them with significance. They are to
be interpreted, it tells us, as premonitions of the goal
of life's pilgrimage, yet tells us also that it is only
through our efforts that life can go forward to that
goal. Hence it offers us a commission in the army of
life, bidding us keep our energies fresh, our appetites
keen, our faculties at cutting edge in its service.

Nor should this appeal to our pride of faculty be despised. Religion, as the mystics have conceived it, calls us to a way of life which the modern world has forgotten, but of which it stands, nevertheless, in urgent need. To keep our faculties keen and our senses fresh, to keep the emotions in check, the spirit unclouded, and to look upon the world with a pure eye is not only the direct approach to another world, but the best passport to happiness in this one. To put the matter at its lowest, it is good worldly as well as other-worldly policy.

Ascetics, if their accounts are to be believed, perceive a more exciting world, and perceive it more intensely than do the rest of us ; they make their sacrifice, and they have their reward. But it is not necessary to be an ascetic to make existing exciting. It is necessary merely to follow certain rules, by the recognition and codification of which mankind has evolved its morals and its religions.

Morals properly regarded are rules of spiritual hygiene, to be cultivated in the interests of intenser living. Sloth, avarice, lechery, gluttony, and anger are hygienically unsound ; by stirring the mud of the passions they dull and trouble the mind. Cultivation of the more elementary sides of our nature inhibits the activity of the higher, and by keeping the mind in agitation prevents us from realising the potentiality for intense spiritual experience that we hold within ourselves. Sin may, in fact, be defined as the refusal to make the most of our possibilities. To sin is to neglect life's challenge to realise all that we have it in us to be ; it is to be content with life at a lower level when we might have enjoyed it at a higher ; it is to opt for the dull and obvious pleasures of traditional experience, rather than for the intense and exciting existence of the spiritual pioneer. Moral health has been wrongly conceived as a form of limitation and restriction ; rightly regarded it is, like bodily health, the attainment of a state of fitness, a fitness of the spirit to register the finer shades of experience, and, like a well-trained instrument, to evolve new and more exquisite harmonies of thought and feeling.

On the religious side, mysticism at its lowest may be regarded as a recognition of the fact that, for those who live in a state of agitation, certain kinds of serene and lasting happiness are impossible. The highest intellectual and creative processes of the human mind are also its most intense experiences. Whatever interferes with them interferes with our pleasures. But the pool cannot reflect the sky when the water is troubled, and mysticism is the practical and systematic cultivation of that mental quietness in which alone the serenest and most intense kind of happiness may be realised ; it is the constant pursuit of that happiness, and as such may be regarded as a set of rules for the attainment of psychological health. This, as I say, is to put the matter at its lowest, but we should be wrong to overlook the significance of the intensity of the experience which mysticism brings. This intensity is bound up with the mystic's conception of the universe, a conception with which, as it seems to me, religion must in future increasingly become identified, and to which it must increasingly subscribe. It is the conception, which only religion can give us, of a goal and purpose for life's pilgrimage, of a world permanent and perfect, beyond the changes and struggles of the life around us, of which, in the recognition of goodness and the appreciation of beauty, we are already beginning to receive our first faint intimations.

It is to this world that religion offers us a direct approach, and in mystical insight reveals it to us, albeit obscurely and in fleeting glimpses, as the goal of our pilgrimage, and revealing, bids us love what it reveals ; I say love, but in the last resort our love, at its highest flood, rushes beyond its object and loses itself in the divine mystery of its object.

Answers to a Questionnaire prepared by the *Nation* on Religious Belief, published in the *Nation* October 16th, 1926.

(1) Answers by readers of the *Nation*.

Question	Numbers answering		
	Yes	No	Doubtful or no answer
1. Do you believe in a personal God ?	743	1,024	82
2. Do you believe in an impersonal, purposive, and creative power of which living beings are the vehicle, corresponding to the Life Force, the *élan vital*, the Evolutionary Appetite, &c. ?	700	892	257
3. Do you believe that the basis of reality is matter ?	506	1,063	280
4. Do you believe in personal immortality ?	807	882	160
5. Do you believe that Jesus Christ was divine in a sense in which all living men could not be said to be divine ?	659	1,136	54
6. Do you believe in any form of Christianity ?	945	796	108
7. Do you believe in the Apostles' Creed ?	393	1,313	143
8. Do you believe in the formulated tenets of any Church ?	453	1,265	131
9. Do you voluntarily attend any religious service regularly ? ..	798	1,021	30
10. Are you an active member of any Church ?	666	1,139	44
11. Do you accept the first chapter of Genesis as historical ?	115	1,685	49
12. Do you regard the Bible as inspired in a sense in which the literature of your own country could not be said to be inspired ?	523	1,268	58
13. Do you believe in transubstantiation?	76	1,731	42
14. Do you believe that Nature is indifferent to our ideals ?	1,081	435	333

(2) Answers by *Daily News* readers.

Question	Numbers answering		
	Yes	No	Doubt-ful or no answer
1. Do you believe in a personal God ?	9,991	3,686	366
2. Do you believe in an impersonal, purposive, and creative power of which living beings are the vehicle, corresponding to the Life Force, the *élan vital*, the Evolutionary Appetite, &c. ?	4,714	6,467	2,862
3. Do you believe that the basis of reality is matter ?	3,049	8,338	2,656
4. Do you believe in personal immortality ?	10,161	3,178	704
5. Do you believe that Jesus Christ was divine in a sense in which all living men could not be said to be divine ?	9,549	4,179	315
6. Do you believe in any form of Christianity ?	10,546	2,879	618
7. Do you believe in the Apostles' Creed ?	7,484	5,071	1,488
8. Do you believe in the formulated tenets of any Church ?	7,299	5,296	
9. Are you an active member of any Church ?	8,796	4,896	351
10. Do you voluntarily attend any religious service regularly ?	10,025	3,822	196
11. Do you accept the first chapter of Genesis as historical ?	5,333	7,488	1,222
12. Do you regard the Bible as inspired in a sense in which the literature of your own country could not be said to be inspired ?	8,950	4,635	
13. Do you believe in transubstantiation?	1,456	12,147	440
14. Do you believe that Nature is indifferent to our ideals ?	5,713	4,987	3,343